D1591202

PUBLICATIONS ON ASIA OF THE
INSTITUTE FOR COMPARATIVE AND
FOREIGN AREA STUDIES

Number 31

Sponsored by
The China and Inner Asia Program of the
Institute for Comparative and Foreign Area Studies
University of Washington
Seattle

The Tale of the Nišan Shamaness

A MANCHU FOLK EPIC

MARGARET NOWAK

Introduction and Interpretation

STEPHEN DURRANT

Translation and Transcription

UNIVERSITY OF WASHINGTON PRESS

Seattle and London

Printed in the United States of America

Library of Congress Cataloging in Publication Data

Nišan shaman-i bithe. English & Manchu.
The tale of the Nišan shamaness.

(Publications on Asia of the Institute for Comparative and Foreign Area Studies; no. 31)
Text of the story in English and in romanized Manchu.
"Sponsored by the China and Inner Asia Program of the Institute for Comparative and Foreign Area Studies, University of Washington, Seattle."
Bibliography: p.
Includes index.
I. Nowak, Margaret, 1944- II. Durrant, Stephen, 1944- III. Washington (State). University. China and Inner Asia Program. IV. Title. V. Series: Washington (State). University. Institute for Comparative and Foreign Area Studies. Publications on Asia; no. 31.
GR336.M36N5713 894'.1 76-49171
ISBN 0-295-95548-1

Contents

Preface

The work of Manchu folk literature presented here lends itself particularly well to an interdisciplinary text-and-context research approach. The tale has had wide appeal among northeastern Altaic peoples, yet with the exception of a somewhat problematic Russian translation, it has never before been translated into a Western language. Thus a purely textual study is essential before any further interpretation can be attempted; the specific considerations and problems of this linguistic aspect will be described in more detail in the first chapter. On the other hand, the context of the tale--a once viable Asian culture where shamanism occupied a central part of the belief system--can best be elucidated by utilizing the insights of anthropology, since this literary work as well as the conditions of its creation, retellings, and final composition into written form are all inextricably linked to the sociocultural setting that made its composition not only possible, but also likely.

Because shamanism has been widely treated

in anthropological literature, a selection of the most promising research approaches must be based not only on definitions and conclusions already made but on an evaluation of the premises and implications of the various studies. For example, this field of inquiry has been investigated for at least a century, and in the course of that time there have certainly been significant readjustments in the anthropological *episteme*, to use Michel Foucault's term. (At the beginning of his "archeological" investigation of the human sciences in Western culture, Foucault defines the *episteme* as "the epistemological field . . . . in which knowledge . . . grounds its positivity and thereby manifests a history which is not that of its growing perfection, but rather that of its conditions of possibility" [1973:xxii]). These changes in orientation and willingness to seek answers in this rather than that domain have not all been historical. Today, for example, we are witnessing opposing epistemological tendencies that are simultaneous rather than chronologically sequential. On the one hand, the increasing sophistication of biochemical research is having profound influences on what would otherwise be narrowly academic debates about whether or not the social sciences are truly "science," merely "scientific," or better off being neither. On the other hand, increasingly refined approaches to the study of symbolic systems--where data are often difficult if not impossible to quantify--now permit anthropologists to perceive the artistic and intellectual creations of other peoples with a greater variety of interchangeable lenses, so to speak, than was ever possible in the days of Frazer's *The Golden Bough*.

Thus a corpus of data like the Manchu shaman tale presented here can stimulate questions in multiple directions. Simply as a written text, it poses problems of authorship, relation to oral tradition, degree of outside influences, internal coherence, and so forth, which not only demand linguistic analysis, but are necessarily related to the wider sociocultural context. As a commentary on the beliefs and practices of shamanism, it opens up further avenues of approach. Depending on the era and perspective, the researcher could focus on shamanism's historical, sociological, psychological, or ideological import. These general summations do not even begin to give an idea of the scope of the literature here: Popov's bibliography on this topic (1932) lists over 650 works on shamanism in Russian alone. For this reason, the present work makes no pretense of being exhaustive in its review of previous studies. What is hoped, however, is that even this limited sampling can elucidate some of the most significant premises and implications of related research, so that the most fruitful approach for investigating the material here can be judged suitable on both on methodological and epistemological grounds.

The book opens with a survey of representative examples of anthropological studies on shamanism, followed by a brief ethnographic and historical background of the tale that includes a discussion of the textual peculiarities of the redaction presented here. Following the translation of the tale is a commentary that attempts to interrelate and interpret both the text and the context. The last chapter is devoted to a critically annotated transcription of the entire handwritten Manchu manuscript.

The authors are especially grateful to Professor Jerry Norman for his constantly available assistance regarding problems of translation. In addition, acknowledgment is also due to Professors Jean-Paul Dumont, Carol M. Eastman, Stevan Harrell, Béla Krigler, Jay Miller, Nicholas N. Poppe, Simon Ottenberg, and Turrell Wylie, who read initial drafts of the manuscript and offered their suggestions, and to Professor Doo Soo Suh, who called attention to and provided the Korean work on this Manchu tale. The authors also wish to thank Harcourt, Brace & World for allowing permission to reprint a portion of T. S. Eliot's "Burnt Norton," from his *Four Quartets*.

Margaret Nowak
Stephen Durrant

THE TALE OF THE NIŠAN SHAMANESS
A MANCHU FOLK EPIC

"Go, go, go, said the bird: human kind
Cannot bear very much reality.
Time past and time future
What might have been and what has been
Point to one end, which is always present."

-- T. S. Eliot
"Burnt Norton," I
Four Quartets

Introduction

Approaches to the Study of Shamanism

A critical survey of approaches to this topic might well begin with a problem related to definition. Early studies mentioning the word *shaman* touched off numerous debates regarding the word's etymology, yet from our vantage point the more significant and far-reaching issue was not the search for origins per se, but rather the underlying implications of the nineteenth-century *Zeitgeist:* concepts of "evolution" and "progress" used as self-evident explanatory principles. The important fact underlying these arguments over etymology was not that the word *shaman* had entered Western vocabularies from Tungusic languages via Russian, but that the term's ultimate origin was being sought in connection with certain presuppositions about the cultures involved. Basically, the alternatives were simple: was the word *shaman* native to Tungusic languages, or could it instead be derived from the Sanskrit word *śramaṇa* "a Buddhist mendicant or ascetic"? The implications of this debate, however, touched on a much broader range of academic problems, and the two chief protagonists in this century were well aware that more was involved here than phonological and lexical reconstruction. In defending the first position, Berthold Laufer points out that the Tungus notion of a shaman is radically different from the referent of the Sanskrit word. He advances his argument to another level, however, when he excoriates the views of "the romantic movement of pan-Indianism" that could give rise to statements such as the one he quotes from A. H. Sayce: "In shamanism, so called from the Shaman or Siberian sorcerer, who is himself but a transformed *çramaṇa*, or Buddhist missionary priest, we rise to a higher conception of religion" [quoted in Laufer 1917:364].

Sergei Shirokogoroff, however, holds that linguistic as well as cultural evidence can indeed support a link between the Sanskrit word and attendant Buddhist concepts and a relatively recent complex of borrowings by the Tungus. Once again the argument stems not so much from etymology per se as it does from Shirokogoroff's ethnographic premises. His article, written as a rebuttal to Laufer's, notes that Laufer sought "to prove the great antiquity of shamanism" (Mironov and Shirokogoroff 1923:110)--an attempt that Shirokogoroff cannot accept, believing as he does that this phenomenon is a recent one in this setting. However, his reasoning regarding the etymology of the word *shaman* is actually not that different from Laufer's in one respect: despite their differing interpretations of various phonological and cultural findings, both men structure their data on the assumption that if only the ultimate origin could be proved and traced, the phenomenon could then be understood.[1]

1. Regarding the etymological debate itself, Nicholas Poppe insists that Laufer's view "is certainly the correct one because *shaman* can hardly be deduced from the Sanskrit *śramaṇa*" (personal communication).

This premise underlies a number of evolutionary studies on shamanism, and it is particularly noticeable in the Russian works, which seek to arrange ethnographic findings in a chronological, deductive sequence. Dimitri Zelenin's book, significantly subtitled *Survivals of Totemism in the Ideology of Siberian Peoples*, is a good example of how an overriding concern for distinguishing temporal stages can result in conclusions that, at the very least, are historical to a disproportionate degree. Zelenin believed that shamanism could be divided into two phases: a prehistory, in which the shaman was only a nature healer, and a later stage, when ecstasy and guardian spirits had come to play a significant role. Tracing the phenomenon back in time,

> Zelenin came to the conclusion that the shaman was originally no less than a kind of totem, more exactly the successor of the totem-animal, which according to his opinion likewise controlled illness demons [Rank 1962:17-18].

Whether or not this conception really did exist in the minds of the Siberian peoples being considered here, tracing shamanism back to totemism sheds little light on the phenomenon as it is integrated within a living group's beliefs and practices. Furthermore, although Zelenin's conclusions appear to be innocuous, a subtle danger exists with this evolutionary approach. Here classifications of "before" and "after" come to imply judgments of moral satisfaction or dissatisfaction, depending upon the researcher's ideological framework; thus designations such as "advanced" and "primitive" can function as loaded terms. This can be noted again and again in early anthropological dicta about "degenerate" religions and "promiscuous hordes." When it appears in Zelenin's work as a correlation made between phases and societal categories ("We can distinguish two different stages of shamanistic religion: 1. shamanism of a primitive communist society and 2. shamanism reflecting the social relations of a class society" [Zelenin 1936:353]), we suspect it to be merely the obligatory bowing to Mecca that appears in any number of reputable Russian works. Nevertheless, the potential for using this approach to bolster one's own conscious or unconscious biases is great. Because of this danger, and considering the limited range of explanations that can be provided by an evolutionary interpretation, there seems to be little value in investigating shamanism by attempting to find its origins and categorize its stages.

Although evolutionism has, at times, been thought of as the direct opposite of diffusionism, this latter approach in anthropology by no means precludes a similar focus on stages of development. As Robert Lowie points out, "to recognize that cultures change in time *and* to see single traits as organically related is to admit the possibility of a definite sequence" (1937:190). Thus a work like Wilhelm Schmidt's twelve-volume diffusionist classic, *Der Ursprung der Gottesidee*, is by no means uninterested in the history of culture change. What Schmidt does deny, however, is universal parallelism; he firmly rejects the idea that all human groups necessarily pass through the same stages. The implications of this premise for the study of both religion and shamanism are twofold. First, Schmidt wanted to prove that very primitive groups could indeed have a "pure" conception of the idea of God; secondly, his denial of unilineal evolution and its attendant notion of universal "progress" led him to focus on "degeneration" as a crucial explanatory principle.

This can be seen clearly in his treatment

of shamanism. He gives copious documentation to describe its artifacts and attendant ideas, but his conclusions and generalizations all focus on the same point: movement away from an earlier, more pristine stage. This emphasis on degeneration can be seen in his treatment of the Inner Asian pastoralists, where he states that

> genuine shamanism is not an integral component of the true ancient religion of these people, and even less is it identical with it. Rather, it represents an extraneous component which did not infiltrate until later developmental stages, and it has considerably transformed their true, ancient nature [1955:617]

Schmidt's concept of shamanism as a degenerate religious phenomenon is thus quite predictable in terms of diffusionist principles. In his evaluation of "black" and "white" shamans, he concludes that black shamanism, which he connects with an ideology focusing on an underworld, and which he would derive from a previously existing agrarian culture complex, is the genuine version, while white shamanism, associated with the shaman's journey to heaven, is only a reaction of the pastoralists. Nevertheless, these correlations and interpretations can be contradicted by empirical evidence (as, for example, that provided by the Yakuts of Siberia, who recognize both black and white shamans), and this fact illustrates the major problem of the diffusionist approach: in attaching so much significance to "logical" historical hypotheses made by the ethnographer, it emphasizes a type of data collecting that merely supports the researcher's original point of view.

A more moderate use of the comparative approach to the study of shamanism can be seen in those studies that seek to explain it as a survival of paleolithic culture or, more specifically, as a derivative of an ancient hunting cult. Proponents of this view, such as Hans Findeisen, consider the presence of animal-helping spirits to be a key feature of the shamanic complex; this in turn is logically traced back to a postulated previously existing hunting cult.

In Findeisen's case this attempt to deduce back in time necessarily involves a preoccupation with chronological correlations. For him

> the shaman is in reality an upper paleolithic magician who has become a shaman. The magical layer in shamanism is generally the oldest; in no case does it become incorporated into shamanism at a later date, but rather it goes back at least to the upper paleolithic age and has been preserved undisturbed in North Asian shamanism from antiquity up to the present, thus for at least 15,000 years [Findeisen 1957:198-99].

Not only is Findeisen's idea of "undisturbed preservation" highly questionable here, but his concern with distinguishing "layers" rather than perceiving the complex as an integrated whole is excessive. Thus he considers it fully justifiable to speak of an animal layer, even though

> hunting magic and animal ceremonies, animal myths and totemic genealogical traditions of the shaman are as good as totally lacking. Such a state of affairs is undoubtedly to be explained chronologically. We observe here that the animal layer and its content must be older than the introduction of the particular culture-pattern which we term shamanism in the exact sense [ibid.:28].

By this it can be seen that Findeisen is

postulating the link between contemporary shamanism and paleolithic culture on the basis of survivals that have themselves all but disappeared. The one remaining feature--animal-helping spirits--is thus used to confirm two hypotheses at once: the previous existence of an elaborate animal layer, which would then affirm the paleolithic hunting cult, and the very link itself between contemporary shamanism and this prehistoric complex.

Findeisen derives empirical evidence for this interpretation from the paleolithic cave paintings of Lascaux, which he connects with a prehistoric shamanism that must have flourished in the Franco-Cantabrian area. This emphasis on paleolithic cave art is further developed in the works of two other investigators of shamanism, Karl Narr and Andreas Lommel. Helmut Hoffmann, who surveys a number of German works on this subject (1967), considers Narr the more cautious of the two on this point: certain recurring motifs or motif complexes such as X-ray representations are almost invariably connected with a shamanistic mentality by Lommel, while Narr evaluates each case on its own merits. Thus, for Narr, the representations of Lascaux Cave are possible as shamanistic pictures, whereas the magicians with antler masks found on the walls of the Cave of Les Trois Frères are not necessarily shaman inspired (Hoffmann 1967:107). In his study, Narr warns that

> one must be extraordinarily cautious about the interpretation of paleolithic masked-dancers as shamans. Since shamanism can be connected with numerous ideologies, it will at times also contain older elements which are found without shamanism, and therefore one should also consider the various forms of animal-imitation related to hunting--and perhaps the representa-

> tion of a higher reality--as a *gestalt* which mixes man and animal. Thus "masked dancers" can, by all means, be shamans, but there are also other possible explanations [1959:252].

Nevertheless, despite his comparatively uncritical interpretations of historic sequences, it is Lommel who ultimately raises the more intriguing and suggestive questions. His beautifully illustrated book (the English translation of *Die Welt der Frühen Jäger: Medizinmänner, Schamanen, Künstler* is titled *Shamanism: The Beginnings of Art*) begins with Findeisen's assumption that

> in shamanism we have, as it were, a concentration of the spiritual essence of hunting, a *gestalt* in which this primitive spirituality is connected and preserved in various regions of the world . . . up to the present day [Hoffmann: 1967:107, quoting Lommel's German edition (1965:23)].

Lommel then explains what he sees as the basis of the world view of these hunters: the belief that every living creature is composed of both a physical and a spiritual aspect, and that separable parts of the body such as bones, skin, and horns, can, because of their link with the spiritual or psychic aspect, be used to bring a creature back to life.

> This intellectual conception, which then becomes a religious one and invents the concept of the "immortal soul," leads in the thinking of the early hunters to tentative attempts to understand, explain, and also to master the world as spiritual life. From this conception there arises art: the picture of an animal contains its soul substance; through the picture a species of animal can be kept alive or brought back to life [Lommel 1967:26].

Although this notion of an intellectual conception "inventing" the religious concept of the immortal soul is dubious, Lommel is at least consistent in his deductive explanation of the connection between shamanism and art.

> Within the framework of this conception of the world there sprang up a particular psychic technique. Attempts were made, in the form of trance, to penetrate into the spiritual world and exercise an influence on it. In the trance the hunter sends out his "soul" to operate in the spirit world. At the same time he takes into himself "souls," so-called "helping spirits," which assist him in his work. The shaman separates his soul from his body and afterwards lets it return, just as in the case of an animal which the hunter kills, the soul is separated from the body and made to enter into a picture and then into another animal [ibid.:26-27].

This kind of preoccupation with animistic concepts "springing up," "arising," and "being invented" is at best a fair reflection of the investigator's world view; at worst it represents a misguided attempt at understanding that uses deductive reasoning to arrive at simplistic interpretations for complex phenomena. This characteristically nineteenth-century approach is certainly not the book's strong point; what is significant about Lommel's work, however, is his suggestion that shamanism on a psychological level is "a technique in which imaginings are transposed into images and then played off against one another," an activation of otherwise unreachable levels of the mind where "the essence of this process of self-healing consists in imposing order and form upon these confused and chaotic images, which threaten to overwhelm the individual" (ibid.:70,64).

Here Lommel is most provocative. Instead

of restricting himself to suppositions about origins and connections, he now raises questions that impinge on the artistic process itself: How does the shaman use artistic form (mime, theater, ventriloquism, song, dance, painting, costuming) to impose order over chaos? For Lommel, one important aspect of the answer to this question concerns the strengthening of the collective psyche, a Durkheimian proposal which he limits to particular cultural situations only. When this psychic technique is activated, however, the group's world view is vitally reaffirmed.

> Psychic images and energies, that is to say traditional ideas or myths of a particular group, can be re-experienced, ordered, intensified, given artistic shape and communicated by means of the trance of an individual specially prepared for this activity [ibid.:148].

In this sense Lommel's equation of the shaman and the artist is far more exciting and open ended than his initial concern for paleolithic cave art as proof of a shamanistic mentality. Few other works on shamanism deal directly with the concept of shaman as creator, intimately involved in the artistic process, although there are numerous studies on such specific topics as the shaman's costume and paraphernalia, versification of shaman songs, and so on.[2] This particular aspect of Lommel's contribution to the

2. The Thirtieth Anniversary Issue of *artscanada, Stones, Bones and Skin: Ritual and Shamanic Art,* is devoted exclusively to shamanism. The lavish illustrations and photographs as well as the written interpretations by various contributors all focus on "that vibrantly interconnected lifeway" in which the shaman is "the balancer, the bringer of equilibrium, the healer, the maker of words, songs, images and forms expressive of the principle of the one in the many, of 'Pan in Proteus'" [1973/1974:31].

study of shamanism thus warrants further consideration: it points to possibilities that are at once stimulating and nonreductionist. Furthermore, some of Lommel's most suggestive statements are those that invite rather than exclude complementary research approaches--for example, his description of the technique of self-healing as a process of "imposing order and form upon confused and chaotic images."

These two opposing concepts--order and chaos--also serve as partial explanations in two articles by Claude Lévi-Strauss. In "The Sorcerer and His Magic," Lévi-Strauss considers the psychological notion of abreaction as the key to understanding how shamanism enables chaotic states, emotions, and representations to be articulated into a whole or system (Lévi-Strauss 1967:176). Then, in "The Effectiveness of Symbols," Lévi-Strauss shifts his attention to a more specific treatment of symbols and system per se, noting how the shaman provides a sick person

> with a *language*, by means of which unexpressed, and otherwise inexpressible, psychic states can be immediately expressed. And it is the transition to this verbal expression--at the same time making it possible to undergo in an ordered and intelligible form a real experience that would otherwise be chaotic and inexpressible--which induces the release of the physiological process [1967a:193].

Such a focus on form and order ultimately prevailing over formlessness and chaos is perhaps the single most recurrent theme to appear in the literature on this topic.

The standard, major work on shamanism, which is probably unexcelled as a generally accessible source of documentation, interpretation, and bibliographic cross references, is

Mircea Eliade's *Shamanism: Archaic Techniques of Ecstasy*. The author is a historian of religion who very carefully sets out his methodological goals and premises in his foreword. He considers his general approach to be inherently concerned with deciphering and revealing the *meaning* of religious phenomena, a task that necessarily involves analysis, interpretation, and comparison. Eliade points out that this last aspect is not rightfully the work of the phenomenologist, and in this way he distinguishes that approach from his own as a historian of religion. Nevertheless, his efforts to "integrate the results of ethnology, psychology and sociology" and "to present a comprehensive view which shall be at once a morphology and a history" (1964:xiii), reveals the close relationship that exists between his approach and phenomenology as a philosophical position.

This latter approach specifies its goals deliberately. It seeks to understand the phenomenon, "that which appears," and this phenomenon is held to be neither purely objective nor purely subjective, but rather "an object related to a subject, and a subject related to an object" (Van der Leeuw 1963:671). This dialectic relation between subject and object (or researcher and data) mutually affecting each other is what constitutes the hermeneutic circle of interpretation. It fundamentally involves history because the process of experiencing a phenomenon and then understanding it necessarily occurs in a temporal sequence. Thus in this approach, interpretative history is of critical importance, and Eliade is vitally interested in discovering, for example,

> why was it possible for such a myth or such a symbol to become diffused? What did it reveal? Why are certain details--often very important ones--lost during diffusion whilst others always survive [Eliade 1961:34]?

With the historian of religion specifically in mind, Van der Leeuw succinctly describes the problem behind such questions: "When he fails to understand, he must describe what he had found, even if he remains at the stage of mere cataloguing" (1963:686).

This is not meant to discredit Eliade's success in assembling and interpreting an immense amount of material. Moreover, his central theme--ritual ecstasy allows the shaman as mediator to reinstate the primordial (*illud tempus*) connection between this world and the world beyond--supports any number of subsequent interpretations that could be carried out using other modes of analysis. What is vaguely unsettling about Eliade's approach, however, is the possibility that it might have the same limitation that characterizes the diffusionist school: an overemphasis on morphological and sequential considerations in data gathering. The following issue, while not of critical importance to Eliade's book as a whole, nevertheless illustrates this particular possibility, and it also leads to some observations on phenomenological research in general.

In his discussion of shamanism in North and Central Asia, Eliade concerns himself with one of the very problems that occupied Schmidt: the distinction between black and white shamans and the attendant correlations of above versus below, and chthonic-infernal versus celestial. Citing Eliade's original French edition (*Le Chamanisme*, 1951), Dominik Schröder regards Schmidt and Eliade in opposition to each other: Schmidt considered black shamanism to be the primary, genuine variety whose ideology focuses on the earth, moon, ancestors, and underworld, whereas Eliade took white shamanism as the genuine, classical form having as its primary characteristic the ecstatic heavenly journey (Schröder 1955:851-52). Thus far the argument seems to be a case of misdirected academic energies: categorizing instead of explaining. But on another level this issue turns into an object lesson in phenomenological methodology.

The revised English edition of *Shamanism* (1964) includes a significant note that not only refers to Schröder's discussion, but more importantly it clarifies its author's priorities in this matter. It will be recalled that Schmidt considered shamanism "a degenerate religious phenomenon characterized by possession," and that the crux of Eliade's whole interpretation of shamanism relates to the shaman's ecstatic journey to another plane of consciousness. Furthermore, the latter's conception of pure, genuine shamanic ideology and practice focuses much more on the quality of the technique than it does on temporal primacy; thus "rudimentary and mechanical means of obtaining trance" are looked upon as aberrant shamanic practices. With this in mind, Eliade expresses the possibility that

> it is perhaps on account of the aberrant kinds of shamanic trance that Wilhelm Schmidt regarded ecstasy as an attitude of "black" shamans only. Since, according to his interpretation, the "white" shaman did not enter into ecstasy, Schmidt did not consider him "a real shaman." . . . In all probability Schmidt denigrated ecstasy because, as a good rationalist, he could not grant any validity to a religious experience that involved "loss of consciousness" [1964:493 n.28].

This quote, with its initially surprising categorization of Father Schmidt as a rationalist, is most instructive as an indication of how phenomenological premises operate in the background of Eliade's methodology. He constantly enters into a hermeneutic relationship with the object he is considering, whether this be morphological data or even another researcher, such as Schmidt. In both cases he is concerned with what these phenomena are saying, that is, what these things, symbols, and people *mean*. The process is ongoing. Changes in interpretation may occur, but never simply as the result of new data. Rather, he will make new data the object of his considerations, and when he believes that he understands, then categorizing gives way to interpretation.

At the very least, Eliade's work cannot be ignored simply because of its vast amount of factual information, but beyond this, the extent to which other investigators will judge this particular approach as valuable depends very much on their own epistemology: how does the research goal of "interpreting meaning," and the morphological classifications that precede this, relate to relevant criteria of valid knowledge?

A totally different approach to the study of shamanism considers it to be a form of psychopathic or social dysfunction. According to such an interpretation, the shaman represents an extreme type of individual characterized by nervous instability or even epilepsy; a variant of this would expect the group that engages in shamanistic activities to be reacting to certain negative environmental conditions:

> A mood of depression, anxiety, or some form of psychological disequilibrium might engulf a people which lived in an immitigable historical situation or in an environment that weighs on the spirit, such as the desert or the Arctic. In such circumstances, shamanistic practices show themselves particularly suited to give a

> feeling of deliverance from unpleasantness [Jensen 1963:215].[3]

This view, which finds greatest expression in the theory of Arctic hysteria as the basis of shamanism, has been espoused by a number of researchers since the nineteenth century, in particular Bogoraz ("K psikologii shamanstva u narodov severovostochnoi Azii":1910), Maria Czaplicka (*Aboriginal Siberia*:1914), and Åke Ohlmarks (*Studien zum Problem des Schamanismus*: 1939). The last work additionally distinguishes between two general geographical types, Arctic and sub-Arctic shamanism. According to Eliade's summary of Ohlmarks's ideas

> shamanism was originally an exclusively Arctic phenomenon, due in the first place to the influence of the cosmic milieu on the nervous instability of the inhabitants of the polar regions. The extreme cold, the long nights, the desert solitude, the lack of vitamins, etc. influenced the nervous constitution of the Arctic peoples, giving rise either to mental illness (Arctic hysteria, *meryak*, *menerik*, etc.) or to the shamanic trance. The only difference between a shaman and an epileptic is that the latter cannot deliberately enter into a trance [1964:24].

Ohlmarks then develops his correlation between the Arctic zone and great shamanizing and the sub-Arctic zone and artificial trance induction. In the first case the shaman is able to enter into a trance state spontaneously; however, the lack of oppressive environmental conditions below the sixtieth degree of latitude necessitates that the shaman in this zone must

3. In fairness to Jensen it should be pointed out that he considers it an oversimplification to derive shamanism exclusively from such factors.

induce a semitrance by artificial means. This small shamanizing, according to Ohlmarks, can occur in one of two forms: it can take place as a mime or imitation, represented by a symbolic ascent of a "cosmic tree," or by the shaman's making the motions of flying; alternatively, it can involve the use of mushroom extract, alcohol intoxication, incense, or other narcotic substances. The underlying characterizations of both categories, however, can be linked with the preoccupations of other approaches: small shamanizing can be connected with degeneration, great shamanizing with dysfunction.

This kind of a focus on group and individual dysfunction is very characteristic of Shirokogoroff's massive monograph, *Psychomental Complex of the Tungus* (1935). Because this work is the primary source of data on the people associated with the Manchu shaman tale to be analyzed here, it is important to note the particular interpretations this author gives to shamanism in its Tungusic setting.

Basically, Shirokogoroff sees this phenomenon as an adaptive response, a safety valve that functions as a vital part of the psychomental complex. Shirokogoroff uses this latter phrase to refer to an organized, self-regulating mechanism that acts to restore equilibrium by stabilizing relations between the individual or group and the environment (ibid.:259,268). Although he denies that shamanism is a psychopathological phenomenon, he does link it with the notion of the instability of individuals and groups.

> Shamanism is very intimately connected with the psychic troubles observed in individuals and masses of ethnic units. . . . These conditions are the cause, in the sense of being stimuli, of the existence of shamanism as a complex, the

> treatment of psychic troubles being the practical aim of shamanism [ibid.:422].

Thus, for Shirokogoroff shamanism is a result of the functioning of the self-regulation psychomental complex, that is, a practical means of restoring equilibrium in cases of overwhelming environmental pressures that can be either natural (a change in the food supply) or cultural (invasions, migrations, and forced assimilation) (ibid.:420).

This accords well with the typical interpretations of Arctic hysteria given by psychological anthropologists. In his attempt to discover what function is served by the symptoms of various non-Western disorders, David Aberle (1952) considers various mental abnormalities found in several Mongol groups (echolalia, echopraxia, coprolalia, startle reaction, phobias). His conclusion, like Shirokogoroff's, focuses on the individual's need to come to terms with the fear of being overwhelmed; thus for Aberle, the symptoms of "so-called arctic hysteria" are basically defense mechanisms (ibid.:296). A similar concern for "the aberrant mental functioning manifested in Arctic hysteria" characterizes Edward F. Foulks's study of this phenomenon among the North Alaskan Eskimo (1972). Here the multiple approaches used attempt to relate anthropological, psychological, and biological factors, reflecting the author's belief that mental symptoms are embedded in a larger network of interacting systems that extend far beyond the individual (ibid.:2).

While Aberle and Foulks are primarily concerned with Arctic hysteria and not shamanism itself, their behavioral orientation is fundamentally the same as that used by Julian Silverman in his article, "Shamans and Acute Schizophrenia" (1967). Although his discussion focuses on shamans "who exhibit the most blatant forms of psychotic-like behavior," including "grossly non-reality oriented ideation, abnormal perceptual experiences, profound emotional upheavals, and bizarre mannerisms" (ibid.:22), Silverman also considers a somewhat more positive possibility: "shamanism is regarded as a total psychological adjustment to a condition of extreme threat, in which one is provided with an alternative to more drastic (i.e., culturally less acceptable) forms of deviancy" (ibid.:25). It is characteristic of Silverman's article that he is constantly moving back and forth between aspects of the shaman's derangement and his cultural support. This is not surprising in view of the equilibrium model he uses to interpret human behavior, nor are his conclusions unlikely or without value in terms of his purpose: examining possible connections between shamanism and psychologists' notions of deviancy and psychotherapy. But it is precisely this choice of psychologists' models rather than the native ones that puts Silverman's investigation squarely in the camp of the Western scientific in-group. The point is not that scientific communicability should be anathema; indeed, successful treatment of Western mental patients benefits from just the opposite attitude. Yet outside of this very limited cultural context, criteria of normalcy, deviancy, and pathology must be expected to exhibit a wide range of variability. To be sure, communication and cooperation between anthropologists and psychologists is to be desired, but the occasional need to use the same terms should never cause the anthropologist to apply psychological labels to cultural data not yet understood on their own terms, within their own system.

Seen in this light, Lucien Sebag's study ("Le chamanisme ayoréo," 1965) illustrates how it is indeed possible to integrate a concern for psychological problems (here, the relationship between the shaman's trance and mental illness) within a much broader anthropological framework. Sebag refuses to generalize beyond his data; he precedes his general conclusions by re-emphasizing that his findings are valid for Ayoréo culture in particular, and are thus not to be directly applied to other societies. Yet he does not eschew cross-cultural comparisons, particularly with other South American groups, nor does he wrench native beliefs out of their symbolic and ideological contexts just to arrive at behavioristic formulations. In fact, his final hypothesis regarding the native view of shamanism is phrased in such a way that psychology becomes a descriptive adjective rather than an ultimate answer. Noting that "a psychological Prometheism" animates this culture (ibid.:119), Sebag concludes that ultimately "a certain vision of the world" that is brought into play in all aspects of Ayoréo life is also responsible for these people's conception of the shaman's activity (ibid.:122). While this might seem overly general and even vague, in the context of the complete study it is a suitable summary, because shamanism is therein treated as but one part of a complex, holistic system that also includes symbolism, mythology, and ideology.

A somewhat different approach to this topic, one that would seek to explain at least some aspects of shamanism in terms of hallucinogenically altered states of consciousness, is nevertheless related to the previous approach because of the similar problem it poses with regard to cross-cultural applicability. The best of these studies are thoroughly documented works that provide pharmacological and ethnobotanical identification for hallucinogenic substances known to be used by shamans in particular cultural settings. One such work is a highly enthusiastic amateur study that has special relevance for the investigation of Siberian shamanism: *Soma, Divine Mushroom of Immortality* (1968). The author, R. Gordon Wasson, attempts to identify the "plant-god Soma" mentioned so often in the ancient Vedic hymns. His finding, the mushroom fly agaric (*Amanita muscaria*), is then linked with a whole range of North Eurasian practices, taboos, and prejudices by means of various types of recorded evidence: linguistic, folkloristic, and travelers' and ethnographers' reports. This last source, which includes notes from the Jesup North Pacific Expedition, seems adequate to support his thesis regarding a fly agaric cult in Siberia. For our purposes, however, what is important about his study is its negative evidence: citing personal communication from the Russian ethnographer Ivan Lopatin, Wasson admits that "the Tungus shamans know nothing of the practice" (ibid.:209 n.1).

In addition to Wasson's basically armchair work, a considerable number of anthropologically researched studies also deal with the relationship between drug ingestion and shamanism. The reader edited by Michael J. Harner (*Hallucinogens and Shamanism*, 1973) is in many ways representative of these. The table of contents reveals a significant geographical pattern here: of the ten articles presented in this book, eight focus on South or Central America, where, it is true, shamanistic activity can unquestionably be linked with hallucinogenic agents. Nevertheless, any general conclusions about this correlation between drug usage and shamanism must remain unsubstantiated outside of this known context. Likewise, problems of validity also arise when a deliberately narrowed approach is moved from its proper object of study and applied to the interpretation of complex wholes on a much larger scale. Harner introduces the last two papers of his book with the thought that perhaps "some generalized biochemical reinforcement" can be found to "underlie regularities in the content of 'other-worldly' experiences and especially widespread and long-persisting fundamental themes in human belief" (ibid.:152,153). Even though this suggestion is posed simply as a hypothesis, Harner shows no intention of searching beyond the boundaries of psychological and behavioristic explanations: the specific psychoanalytic and biochemical possibilities he considers include "oral aggressive phenomena" and "genetically-based fear-cues or images which have been biochemically stimulated" (ibid.). Without denigrating the value of all reductionism, it should nevertheless be pointed out that an anthropological approach that seeks answers in the realm of biochemistry is, by virtue of its stated or implied epistemology, ill-equipped to consider such qualitatively charged phenomena as belief systems, symbolism, ideology, and so on.

A less restricted orientation is shown in a short research paper by Richard Shweder, who focuses on the shaman as a person with unique cognitive capacities. Using a carefully constructed research design, Shweder was able to compare individual and group responses for two matched groups (shamans and nonshamans) who were "presented with and forced to confront concrete examples of chaos, i.e., diffuse, unstructured stimuli" (1972:402). In the experiment, both groups were shown six series of photographs--seventy-two pictures in all--whose subjects appeared in twelve gradations of clarity: from a complete blur to a perfectly defined focus. They were then asked to look carefully at each photograph and then either tell the examiner what it represented, or simply say "I don't know." For three of the six series, three possible responses were also suggested to the participants.

What is significant about Shweder's research is that it ultimately sought to consider its findings in the light of native Zinacanteco ideology. Thus he found that the results confirmed the native point of view: the shaman has extraordinary cognitive (here "perceptual" is also implied) capacities.

> Shamans are significantly different from nonshamans in three aspects of cognitive style. . . . First, shamans avoid bafflement more than nonshamans. They are imposers of form on diffuse sense data. Second, shamans are more productive in their responses; they are more generative of different responses. Third, shamans seem to have available to themselves their own constructive categories and remain relatively insensitive to the alternative categories provided by the experimenter [ibid.].

As this article is intended to be an introductory study, Shweder does not proceed to any conclusions about the relationships between these cognitive capacities, role experience, and pre-existing personality. Nevertheless, despite this paper's brevity, Shweder's approach warrants further consideration. His thesis that "the shaman emerges as an agent of . . . control and order who tames the wild by placing it in a cultural framework" (ibid.:408), links him with those investigators who would study both cognition and creativity. Moreover, his particular experiment leads to the observation that at least some of these data on shamanism can be measured on a level other than that of the most radical biological reductionism.

A further, incidental aspect of Shweder's study is also significant: it is published in an anthropological reader devoted to the study of religion. This fact points to an often unrecognized difficulty concerning investigations of both religion and shamanism: labels such as *religion, shamanism, soul,* and *spirit* tend to be used with such imprecision and even arbitrariness by social scientists that research in these areas frequently lacks communicability. Overt examples of this occur frequently in the literature. Findeisen contends that shamanism is indeed a religion, but then makes the immediate qualification that "this all more or less depends on how we define 'religion' in general" (1957:200). The widely used watchword of nineteenth-century ethnology--animism--merely Latinizes the word for "soul" without making the issue any clearer. Thus definitions like the following for "shamanism" become tautologies: "a stage of religious development which corresponds to animism as both the philosophy and the theology of shamanism" (Bogoraz 1910:1-2).

A way of dealing with such problems--which can be seen to stem either from arbitrary ad hoc definitions or an excessive concern for specifying morphological components--is suggested in a work by Clifford Geertz in which he proposes a twofold approach to the study of religion: "first, an analysis of the systems of meaning embodied in the symbols which make up the religion proper, and, second, the relating of these systems of social-structural and psychological processes" (1971:42). Although the implications of this approach would appear to be promising indeed, it should first be pointed out that within the context of the work referred to above, Geertz refers to shamanism as a "desiccated type" of folk/tribal religious tradition, calling the very designation "shamanism" one of those "insipid categories by means of which ethnographers of religion devitalize their data" (ibid.:39). Responding to this specific charge, a historian of religion defends the use of such labels: "But surely we need a morphology of religion, a definition system of terms and concepts of manifest religious phenomena, if we shall at all understand the subject we are dealing with" [Hultkranz 1970:351].

The debate here stems from two different approaches to the study of meaning. Geertz wants to focus on the interpretation of symbolic forms, grounding his investigations of systems of meaning in the concrete facts of social interaction and events. Hultkranz, on the other hand, is much more atomistic in his approach; he fears relinquishing discrete terms, features, and definitions because of his implicit assumption that meaning is most adequately comprehended by adding form to form and then summing up the results. Since the literature on shamanism includes research based on both approaches, we should consider the valid points in each argument. To delimit the field of study unambiguously, research on such a variously interpreted topic as shamanism must at least implicitly deal with definitions of terms and concepts. Nonetheless, such a study would lose much by refusing to go beyond an atomistic concern for features and forms. While such an approach can certainly serve as a starting point, a morphological indication of the breadth or narrowness of the topic under consideration, an exclusive concern for features and definitions is simply unable to deal with shamanism, or any other integrated topic, as a holistic system of meanings. A more fruitful approach would take both points into consideration, beginning with a morphological as well as a real delimitation of the topic, but extending the focus of study, not only to the symbolic forms themselves, but also to their social and psychological correlatives.

In this light, then, the following general characteristics are presented as being typical of shamanism in the context of Northeast Asia:

(1) a trance or ecstatic state that the shaman is able to induce himself (unlike epileptic seizures); (2) a group-held belief that some nonphysical component of the shaman's being either "leaves" or "empties itself" so that the shaman can serve as the instrument of some other dimensional reality; (3) a period of training, initiation, or near madness prior to public acknowledgment of the shaman's status; (4) a social, rather than an individual motivation for achieving a trance state;[4] and (5) a fundamental concern for righting something that has gone awry, that is, a reaffirmation of cosmic or microcosmic order over whatever form of chaos is threatening to overwhelm the group or individual concerned.

Before further developing this definition of shamanism as it occurs in this particular cultural setting, it should first be pointed out that this deliberate geographical limitation of the phenomenon to the narrow or classical north Asian area of shamanism is concomitantly reflected in the sampling of the works that have been surveyed above. While it is true that these studies were not all so restricted geographically, this survey makes no claims to be exhaustive, particularly as related topics such as divination, curing, and sorcery were hardly mentioned except as they occurred in otherwise relevant quotations. For the purpose of understanding the Manchu frame of reference of the tale presented here, however, it is not necessary to consider every aspect of a broad definition of the phenomenon; in fact, it makes much more sense heuristically to restrict the

4. Hoffmann [1967:103] makes this a sine qua non for shamanism, pointing out the difference between the mystic who experiences ecstasy for his own sake and the shaman whose ecstasy serves a social system--fetching game for the clan hunters, bringing back the escaped soul of a sick person, etc.

term *shamanism* in this case to the emic core of the definition presented above: the mediation of a mundane problem and a supernatural solution by means of an ecstatic journey that literally goes out of this world.

This key concept of mediation is fittingly polycontextual in its explanatory power. The tale deals with the adventures of a female shaman who bridges the critical gap between the land of the living and the kingdom of the dead. Like the nucleus of a concentric series of circles, this kernel of a literary plot can be set within ever widening cultural and theoretical contexts, each further expanding the mediation theme. In the first case, the cultural setting of the tale amplifies the concept in other domains besides plot, setting, and characters--notably the Manchu norms of kinship and social propriety, where relationships that initially appear irrevocably polarized (e.g., husband's clan / wife's clan; old widower / young widow) can be seen, upon closer inspection, to intersect at certain critical junctures. In the second case, mediation occurs frequently--either explicitly or implicitly--as a pivotal concern of numerous anthropological studies of shamanism. This is particularly the case with the order / chaos opposition so often noticed by researchers of various persuasions. Whether viewed behavioristically, cognitively, or symbolically, the shaman is seen by them as an ambiguous individual, neither completely normal nor completely deviant, one who spans the gap between sanity and insanity, bafflement and certitude, this world and the world beyond--and thereby is able to make sense out of whatever non-sense threatens to annihilate interpretation.

A final extension of this theme of mediation would take it beyond the particulars of literary tale and cultural context into the realm of logically based theory. Structural anthropology, whose goal is "to discover, behind the chaos of rules and customs, a single structural scheme existing and operating in different spatial and temporal contexts" (Lévi-Strauss 1967:22), utilizes the concept of mediation to describe the same type of logical event as would generally characterize the examples given above: two related terms are brought together by an ambiguous but relevant middle term. While a thorough and complete structural analysis of the Manchu shaman tale would be impossible here due to insufficient cultural data, it would still appear worthwhile to consider this material in the light of some of the insights of structural anthropology, so as to indicate the direction such an analysis could take if more information were available.

Let us conclude these remarks on methodological approaches and their implications for specific data by recapitulating the research concerns that have been judged most suitable for our purposes. First, this study, which is deliberately restricted to a narrow and particular sociocultural context, should nonetheless attempt to deal with the problem holistically, rather than in an atomistic fashion. Even though it is not always possible to document every aspect of the text's social, psychological, and ideological correlations, this does not obviate the need to integrate as much data as possible into an interconnected system. Finally, the unifying focus of this study--the concept of mediation--should appear as a recognizable pattern no matter how the text is viewed: whether as a closed universe made up of plot, setting, and characters; as a literary remnant of a once viable and unique culture in which shamanism was a critical part of the belief system; or as a corpus of data that, in its logical organization, can be seen to mirror the unconscious structural scheme underlying the whole of Manchu culture.

The Cultural Context of the Tale

This tale of the Nišan shamaness is an original example of native Manchu folk literature that can be geographically linked with the Heilung-chiang region of eastern Asia--an area generally south of Siberia and the Amur River, east of Mongolia, northeast of China proper and northwest of present-day Korea. The text's mention of the Ming dynasty (1368-1644) and the Tai-tsung Emperor (r. 1626-1643) gives an approximation of the time of composition, although as a product of folk literary tradition its authorship is unknown.

The setting of this tale is greatly affected by the historical relation existing between Manchuria, with its native Altaic (specifically Tungusic) language and culture, and China, the vast, assimilating empire. First of all, the word *Manchu* itself should be clarified. Lattimore has noted that there was no inclusive Chinese term for Manchuria that held good for all periods as the name Manchu was only institutionalized about the time of the creation of the Ch'ing dynasty in 1644 (1967:105). This era lasted until 1911 when the whole system of dynastic rule, which had been administered for the past 267 years by the Manchus, was overthrown by the revolution that brought a republican system of government to China.

Evidence for the existence of a living Manchurian language and culture distinct from the Chinese is tenuous at best. Nevertheless, latest available statistics cite 2,410,000 Manchus and 19,000 Sibe living in the People's Republic of China (*Hsin-hua tzu-tien* 1958: appendix 15:17). This latter group (also referred to as "Sibo," "Sibintsi") is significant for purposes of comparison: resettled in the eighteenth century in the Ili region of

Sinkiang, these Tungusic people "have retained their ancestral language, while those who remained in Manchuria became completely sinified in the course of time" (Norman 1974:159). Thus "it appears that the Sibe are now the only speakers of anything that can be called Manchu" (ibid.), and as such they can presumably supply data that would be less influenced by the effects of linguistic and cultural assimilation than the groups that remained in Manchuria.

It is important to recognize the pattern of conquest and assimilation as it occurred in the Chinese dynastic system. When the Manchus conquered China and established the Ch'ing dynasty, they were acting as non-Chinese rulers over the Middle Kingdom--a vast, populous, and bureaucratically organized empire. Such "barbarians" ruled the country

> with Chinese help and made little effort to change Chinese ways--so little, in fact, that they may be regarded, especially in the case of the Manchus, as integral parts of the Chinese political order [Fairbank in Reischauer and Fairbank 1960:243].

This capsule summary of the "assimilation theory" is more critically developed by Franz Michael, whose book, *The Origin of Manchu Rule in China*, stresses the belief that acculturation, particularly in matters of political philosophy and organization, must have taken place in the conqueror's home territories prior to the conquest itself (Michael 1942:3). No matter how assimilation is interpreted, however, it always involves some degree of tension between two different ways of life. While this may not be equally noticeable in all cultural contexts, the practice of shamanism was one area that was of particular concern to the Manchu Ch'ien-lung Emperor (r.1736-1795), since this part of his native tradition was already showing unmistakable signs of decline and disintegration. This ruler's attempted solution of the problem made use of the Manchu writing system that had been invented a century and a half before he commissioned a six-volume work, *Hesei toktobuha manjusei wecere metere kooli bithe (Book of Laws for Manchu Sacrifices and Offerings Established by Imperial Command)*, for the purpose of preserving the "correct" forms, words words, and rituals of shamanism. As Shirokogoroff points out, "it is evident that at Ch'ien-lung's time the rites needed both corrections and artificial preservations because of loss of language" (1935:204). But

> the formalization of Manchu ritual did not occur on genuine soil. In fact, by his time the Imperial Family was already under a strong Chinese influence, and what is found in the book of rites is not an exact picture of the original Manchu complex [ibid.].

In addition, even if the loss of language and custom had taken place entirely within Manchu culture, the very act of committing a living tradition to written forms would still have had the effect of stifling spontaneous creation and vitality. This is precisely what happened in the case of the written records kept of the spirits and the rites connected with shamanism. Shirokogoroff, who terms this "petrification" or "fixation," states that

> the effect of the fixation of spirits, prayers, and rituals was that the shamans who wanted to introduce innovations required by the change of psychological conditions and implied by the existing and everchanging theories concerning the spirits, or who wished to drop some of the elements which might become a simple burden in the complex, could not do it. The specialists in shamanism, referring to the written records,

> required a particular strictness: since the old shamans did so, the new ones must do the same [ibid.:342].

Thus even a native Manchu work--*The Book of Laws*--cannot be regarded as a totally satisfactory source of information on the subject of living, indigenous shamanism in that setting. The same reservations likewise apply to two books based on the above: Louis Langlès, *Rituel des Tatars-Mantchoux* (1804) and Charles de Harlez, *La religion nationale des Tartares Orientaux* (1887). Other sources are also limited: a small number of fragmentary shaman songs in Manchu collected by Andrei Rudnev and re-examined by Vilmos Diószegi (1960); two Russian sources, "New Data on Living Manchu Speech and Shamanism" by Rudnev (1912); "Short Notes on the Present-day Status of Shamanism among the Sibo Living in the Ili Region and Tarbagatay" by N.N. Krotkov (n.d.); as well as Shirokogoroff's ethnographic works on the Tungus.

Shirokogoroff is the primary ethnographer of these North Asian peoples, and his monograph, *Psychomental Complex of the Tungus* (1935), is without question the most complete source of data, for it describes almost every conceivable aspect of their life. Yet the very title of this tome suggests that caution should be used before accepting his occasionally convoluted theories and interpretations. Shirokogoroff at times waxes eloquent in his own behalf, yet the dates and circumstances of his research are such today that he can be neither confirmed nor countered with contrary evidence. The sheer volume and specificity of his data is at times overwhelming and for that reason Shirokogoroff's works may certainly be treated as primary sources. Nevertheless one must also take into account his occasional substitution of strongly expressed personal opinion for trained, unbiased ethnographic reporting.

From the literary point of view, the shaman tale translated here is noteworthy on two counts. First, in all its redactions, it represents, according to Shirokogoroff, the only native document on indigenous Manchu shamanism (ibid.:308). Second, the history of this particular version of *Nišan shaman-i bithe* is especially interesting because of its relation to other redactions.

The version presented here has been translated previously: into Russian by Maria Petrovna Volkova (1961) and into Korean by Seong Baeg-in (1974). Because the present English translation was made from the photoreproduction of the Manchu manuscript appearing in Volkova's edition, her preface will serve to summarize the text's background.

The written story of the Nišan shamaness was discovered, according to Volkova, by A.V. Grebenshchikov (1880-1941), an instructor of Manchu language and literature at the Oriental Institute in Vladivostok. Having heard of the existence of the legend from P.P. Schmidt, Grebenshchikov set out in 1908 to travel through Manchuria in order to find copies of this story. Although the tale was very popular in northern Manchuria among Manchus, Solons, and Dahurs, it was transmitted orally, and written versions were hard to find. Nevertheless, in the next few years Grebenshchikov did succeed in acquiring three written copies of the text.

The first, acquired from a Manchu named Jingkeri, Grebenshchikov designated as the Tsitsikar manuscript, since it came from a village not far from that city. This redaction is short, consisting of only twenty-three pages, five lines per page, and Volkova notes that "it does not appear complete." The story recounted in the Tsitsikar manuscript begins with a description of servants returning from a hunt with news of the death of an official's beloved son, and concludes with the scene of a bargain made between the shamaness and an underworld figure regarding this reanimated boy's life-span.

The second redaction was acquired by Grebenshchikov near Aigun in 1909. It is more complete, consisting of fifty pages, twelve lines per page. Like the Tsitsikar manuscript, this account also lacks the beginning and ending of the third redaction. It is significant to note Volkova's observation that "the episode of the destruction of the shamaness' paraphernalia is consigned to a single sentence"--in marked contrast to the third redaction where the denouement includes a civil deposition carried out in accordance with Chinese bureaucratic procedures.

This third redaction, acquired by Grebenshchikov in 1913 and written down in Vladivostok by a Manchu named Dekdengge, is the one translated here since it is the most complete text available.[5] Dekdengge's handwritten manuscript (reproduced in photocopy and appended to Volkova's edition) presents a number of interpretative difficulties. In the first place, his cursive script is occasionally ambiguous. For example, the letter complex *-ngk* or *-ngg-* is often written so that it can also be read and transcribed simply as *-ng-* or even *-ik-*. In the present work, such orthographic ambiguities are treated by assuming that the standard spelling was intended.

A more difficult problem occurs in cases where unambiguous spellings do not correspond to standard written Manchu. Such "accidentals" can be grouped together into categories:

5. Shirokogoroff [1935:44, 284] mentions an epic poem by the same name that contains over nine thousand Manchu words, but we have no way of checking on the present-day existence of this text.

intervocalic stops often become fricatives (e.g., VbV → VfV; VgV → VhV); the back -ū- vowel is not consistently distinguished from -*o*-, and so on. These types of spelling errors are instructive in that they consistently occur in predictable phonological patterns. However, standard written forms occasionally alternate with these irregular spellings: for example, standard written Manchu *fayangga* ("soul") is generally spelled *fainggo* in the text, but *fanangga* also occurs sporadically. This indicates that Dekdengge was familiar with standard written Manchu as a learned tradition; yet his own language, presumably a Manchu dialect, differed from the older phonological system, which is reflected in the classical Manchu script. This difference is presumably responsible for his characteristic spellings.

These orthographic inconsistencies and ambiguities coupled with the occasional occurrence of words not found in the standard lexicographic sources make the text difficult to decipher in a number of places. The two previous translators of this text differ in their handling of such problems. Volkova transcribes the nonstandard cursive forms into Cyrillic representations of what she considers to be their standard equivalents. She does this, however, without providing footnotes to justify her interpretation. Nevertheless, her Russian translation was of great help in the initial stages of this project. Her transcription and translation were compared word-for-word with the developing English translation, and her interpretations more than once suggested a fruitful way out of an otherwise blind alley. The second translation, Seong Baeg-in's Korean study of the same work (also based on Dekdengge's manuscript), treats the problem of nonstandard forms with more thoroughness. His romanized transcription reproduces all original spellings as accurately as possible; then he suggests standard equivalents and interpretations for unusual lexical items. In addition, Seong's work gives a complete listing and categorization of the predictable spelling errors that occur in the original Manchu text.

The transcription that appears at the end of this work was thus made after the two previous interpretations were studied, and the footnotes reflect this accordingly.

It should be re-emphasized that this definition of shamanism is not meant to be applied beyond the areas of Manchuria, Mongolia, Siberia, and Central Asia--the loci of "classical" shamanism. Nor is the sampling of works surveyed exhaustive: such related topics as divination, curing, and sorcery have hardly been mentioned.[6]

6. The definition problem is handled very thoroughly by Johan Reinhard (pp. 12-20) in a recent and very relevant anthology that only became available as this book was in press: *Spirit Possession in the Nepal Himalayas*, edited by John T. Hitchcock and Rex L. Jones (New Delhi: Vikas Publishing House, 1976).

Translation of the Text

In the time of the Ming Dynasty there was a village called Lolo where there resided a *yuwan wai* official[1] named Baldu Bayan.[2] His household lived in immense wealth and his servants, horses, and mules were immeasurable. In his middle years a son was born to him. Upon reaching the age of fifteen, this boy one day took the household servants to go hunting at Heng Lang Mountain. Along the way he became ill and died. 1

Thereafter, the official and his wife, worried because they were without descendant, did only good. They repaired and built temples,

1. *Yuwan wai* (Chinese *yüan-wai* 员外) is an official title acquired by purchase. Thus it became a frequent designation for the wealthy, and as such it will be translated hereafter simply as "official" [Morohashi 1955-60:2:1010].

2. Later in the story Baldu Bayan is referred to as being a member of the *bayara* clan. This word alone means "to be rich," and *bayan* is a related word meaning "rich, rich man." On the bayara clan, see Shirokogoroff [1924:20].

knelt to seek mercy from Buddha, and prayed to the gods. Taking candles and fragrant incense, they burned these in one place after another.
2 Also, they aided the poor, supported orphans, and took care of widows. Since the good they did was becoming renowned, heaven had pity on them, and even though they were fifty years of age a son was born to them. They were very pleased, and because he was born in their fiftieth year, they named him Sergudai Fiyanggo.[3] They loved him like a precious pearl and raised him without letting him out of their sight.

When Sergudai reached the age of five, his parents saw that he was clever of mind and clear of speech, so they summoned a teacher for him. At home the teacher instructed him in reading and writing, and he also made him practice the military arts--foot archery and mounted archery. The sun and moon went by in a blur as swiftly as an arrow in flight, and Sergudai reached fifteen years of age. One day, having met his father and mother, he suddenly made a request: "I
3 would like to go out hunting to try the archery I've learned. I wonder what you, father, would think about this?"

To his son's request the father responded, "Before your time there was an older brother. At the age of fifteen he went to hunt at Heng Lang Mountain where he passed away. I really don't think I should let you go."

At this Sergudai Fiyanggo replied, "I was born in the human world as a male, yet I have gone nowhere. Will I eternally guard the house? None of us escapes the fate that comes bringing life and death to us all."

3. *Sergudai* is a common Manchu name for men. *Fiyanggo* (standard written Manchu *fiyanggū*) means "the youngest, the last."

After Sergudai said this the official had no alternative but to agree, saying, "If you insist on going hunting, take Ahalji and Bahalji and go! But don't be gone long. Be careful and return quickly. And do not disregard the thoughts I expressed previously!"

4

Sergudai Fiyanggo agreed to his father's instructions and immediately called Ahalji and the other servants, commanding, "Tomorrow we are going hunting. Line up the people, horses, and saddles. Prepare the weapons, bows and arrows, and put the tent into the wagon. Feed the falcons and striped dogs well and get them ready!"

Upon his saying this Ahalji and Bahalji agreed and hurriedly went to make preparations. The next day Sergudai Fiyanggo took leave of his father and mother in the traditional manner, and having mounted a white horse, he ordered Ahalji and the others to follow. Carrying the falcons on their shoulders and leading the striped dogs, all the servants, bearing quivers, bow cases, bows and arrows, formed rows in front and behind Sergudai. The procession of wagons and horses, one after the other, was very festive and magnificent. All the people of the village, young and old alike, came outside to watch, and every- 5 one marveled, praising and extolling him.

Since all the hunters went with great speed, whipping their horses, they arrived in an instant at a mountain renowned for hunting. Thereupon they pitched their tents, and digging a cooking hole, they placed a pot on it. After Sergudai left the cook behind to make the meal, he took all the servants and commanded Ahalji and Bahalji, "Let's set out the battue lines, encircle the mountain, and hunt."

Then, having set out the battue, some shot their arrows and others stabbed with their spears. Releasing the hawks and setting the dogs, they let them give chase. They shot at the various birds and beasts, and in every case there was not a single one they did not obtain.

Just when they were happily hunting, Sergudai Fiyanggo's body suddenly became cold all
6 over, and then at once it became feverish. Since his head had become dizzy and he was feeling sick, he immediately called to Ahalji and Bahalji, "Quickly gather in our battue lines; I'm not well!"

Frightened, they hurriedly gathered in the battue and came to the tent. After putting their young master inside, they lit a fire. They were about to warm him by the fire in order to make him sweat, but he was already sweating so heavily from his fever that it was not suitable to expose him to the heat, so instead the servants felled a mountain tree, made a litter, and laid their young master down on it.

The servants took turns carrying the litter and set out toward home as if flying. Sergudai Fiyanggo, weeping, said, "I think the condition of my illness is serious. I no longer know if I
7 will be able to reach home. Ahalji and Bahalji, let whichever one of you brothers who is willing go home quickly and take the news to my father and mother. Please clearly pass on my words to them for me: 'I myself am unable to repay the kindness of your having lovingly raised me. I had thought that I would mourn for you as a filial son only after you reached one hundred years of age. Who would have known? Since heaven is destroying me and I have arrived at my fated time, I will not be able to see you again. In the blink of an eye I am going to die, a young man!' Tell them, 'Do not mourn excessively, father and mother. It is important that you take care of yourselves at your age. All this is nothing more than the predetermined reckoning

of the fate we are accorded. Please observe the right time for mourning and weeping.'"

Having said, "Please clearly pass on my words . . ." he was about to speak again, but he was unable to open his mouth. His jaw locked and no words came from him; his chin tilted upward and his eyes became fixed. 8

After his breathing had stopped, Ahalji, Bahalji, and the others gathered around his litter, and the mountains and valleys all echoed to the sounds of their weeping. Then Ahalji stopped weeping and said to them all, "The young master is already dead and we will not be able to revive him by weeping. It is important that we take the corpse and begin our journey. Bahalji, take everyone with you; treat the corpse of our young master respectfully and slowly proceed home with it. I will go ahead with ten horsemen and report the news to the official. We will prepare the things in the home for the young master's funeral." 9

Ahalji then took the others, and riding his horse, reached the gate of the house in an instant, for he rode home as swiftly as if he were flying. After he dismounted, he entered the house and knelt down before the old official, but then he merely wept in a loud voice and said nothing at all. The old official was upset and scoldingly said, "Servant, what is wrong? You went off to hunt; why have you come back in tears? I assume your young master sent you ahead with some important matter. Why do you weep and say nothing?"

When he asked time after time and Ahalji kept on crying and did not answer, the official became angry and scolded him: "You petty slave! Why do you just stand here crying without making your report? Will the matter be brought to an end by your weeping?" 10

After he said this, Ahalji stopped weeping,

knelt down and said, "The young master became ill during our journey and met his end. I have come ahead to bring the news."

The official, who had not paid close attention, asked, "What ended?"

Ahalji answered, "No, the young master himself has died."

As soon as the official heard these words it was as if a clap of thunder had exploded above his head and he screamed, "Dear son!" and at once fell on his back.

At this the old lady hurriedly came running, and when she questioned Bahalji, he replied, "After having heard the news I came to report, namely that the young master has died, he fainted like this and fell."

11 Having heard this, the old lady was stupefied as if lightning had flashed before her eyes, and after she called out, "Mother's son!" she fainted and fell right across the old man. The servants, having taken fright at this, stood them up, and only then did they revive.

Everyone in the household wept when they heard what had happened and all the villagers gathered at this sound of weeping. Just at the point when all were loudly weeping together, Bahalji entered in tears, kowtowed to the official and reported, "I have arrived with the body of the young master."

The official and his wife, together with the villagers, met the body of the young master outside of the gate. After they brought it into the house they placed it on a bed. Everyone crowded around, and all heaven and earth shook at the sound of their sobbing. After they had 12 cried for a while everyone advised, "Rich sir, you two elderly people, why weep like this? Once one has died, even though you weep, is there a way to revive him? You ought to prepare the coffin and other things for the corpse."

After this was said, the official and his

wife finally stopped crying and said, "Your words are quite correct. Nevertheless, I still grieve and am truly unable to endure it in my mind. My dear, clever son has died! Beyond this what do I regret? Simply this: Would that there lived a son to whom I could leave my property!"

The official then called Ahalji and Bahalji and said, "This servant only opens his mouth and weeps. Prepare for your young master the seven **13** funeral offerings,[4] the lead horses, and the treasuries. Spare nothing!"

Ahalji and Bahalji stopped weeping and obeyed the commands. When they reported that they had prepared for the young master ten dappled, flower-patterned lead geldings, ten sorrel geldings the color of fire, ten light bay geldings the color of gold, ten fast chestnut geldings, ten white geldings, and ten black geldings the color of ink, the official then ordered, "Have them load sacks of various brocade clothing on the backs of thirty horses and make them load the rest of the horses with quivers and bow cases. Take down the red saddle and red bridle decorations and finish saddling the snow-white, dark-maned horse with a gold-plated bridle. Lead the way!" 14

Then he called the herdsmen and said, "Bring from the herds ten cows, sixty sheep, and seventy pigs. Slaughter all of these and prepare them."

Ahalji and the herdsmen responded "Yes, sir!" and each went to make preparations. The official called his women servants Aranju and Saranju and said, "You two take all the women of the village who will help and immediately finish

4. Volkova considers this a reference to the "seven precious things"--enumerated differently in various Buddhist sources--here probably consisting of gold, silver, rubies, pearls, kumiss, amber, and coral.

preparing seventy loaves of wheat cake, sixty loaves of buckwheat cake, fifty twisted cakes, forty twisted buckwheat cakes, ten bottles of liquor, ten pairs of geese, twenty pairs of 15 ducks, thirty pairs of chickens, and two tables of each of the five fruits. If you delay I will beat you all!"

All answered "Yes sir!" and each left to make preparations. In no time at all they were busily carrying all these things, arranging them so that they filled the courtyard. The quantity looked as high as a cliff, the various kinds of meat were piled up like a mountain, the liquor was put out and poured forth like an ocean, and the tables of fruit and bread were lined up one after another in rows. After the gold, silver, and paper money from the treasuries were arranged in great abundance, all the people sprinkled the liquor around and cried. Then from the side the official wept, saying,

Father's prince, *ara*
one born *ara*
in the fiftieth year! *ara*
Sergudai Fiyanggo! *ara*
When I saw you *ara*
16 I greatly rejoiced. *ara*
Who will inherit *ara*
these many horses *ara*
and herds of cattle and sheep? *ara*
I relied greatly *ara*
upon the prince's grandeur, *ara*
intelligence, and purity. *ara*
What prince will sit astride *ara*
the riding horses? *ara*
Although there are servants, *ara*
what master will order them about? *ara*
Although there are hawks, *ara*
who will receive them? *ara*
Although there are striped dogs, *ara*
what child will lead them? *ara*

When he was sobbing like this, the mother also said,

Mother's clever prince! *ara*
For the sake of my own offspring *ara*
I did good deeds *ara*
and prayed for good fortune. *ara*
Wise, *ara*
pure prince, *ara*
deft of hand, *ara*
adroit prince, *ara*
you were born in my fiftieth year!
ara
Beautiful in form, *ara*
fair prince, *ara*
learned, *ara*
with soft voice! *ara*
Wise prince, *ara*
upon what son now *ara*
can I depend and live? *ara*
One who was kind to the servants, *ara*
imposing prince, *ara*
prince of comely form! *ara*
Your complexion and nature *ara*
was like that of P'an An.[5] *ara*
Beautiful prince! *ara*
When mother went strolling *ara*
in the street *ara*
you were like a hawk! *ara*
I seek to hear *ara*
your voice. *ara*
When you went into the valley *ara*
there was the sound of bells. *ara*
Mother's beautiful son! *ara*

17

5. Seong notes that this word is a loan from Chinese and attempts to relate it to the names of several musical instruments [1974:40]. However, P'an An is probably an abbreviated name of P'an An-jen 潘安仁, a man of the Chinese Chin Dynasty (265-419 A.D.) who was renowned for his physical beauty. His biography appears in *Chin Shu* 晉書 [Records of the Chin Dynasty], vol. 55.

What son will I look upon now? *ara*
I live cherishing you! *ara*

Then falling on her back, froth came out of her mouth, and falling on her stomach, saliva flowed, and she spit mucous into a tub. As she 18 was crying her tears flowed into a veritable river. At this point an old man, an almost dead hunchback who walked all bent over, arrived at the gate and called out,

Deyangku, deyangku Guards of the gate
Deyangku, deyangku listen!
Deyangku, deyangku Go to your master
Deyangku, deyangku and please tell him
Deyangku, deyangku that a dying old man
Deyangku, deyangku has come
Deyangku, deyangku to the outside of the gate
Deyangku, deyangku Please say
Deyangku, deyangku that I would like to see him.
Deyangku, deyangku As a small token
Deyangku, deyangku I would like to burn the paper.[6]

When he finished making this request the gate guards went in and reported it to Baldu 19 Bayan. The official said, "How pitiful! Bring him in quickly. Let him eat from the mountain of meat and cakes we have offered for the young master, and let him drink from the ocean of wine."

At this the gate guards ran out and brought in the old man. When he came in he did not notice the meat, cakes, and wine for the offering, but instead went directly past this and stood near the coffin of the young master. He leaned his hand on the coffin, hopped up and down, and cried in a high voice, saying in sobs,

6. This refers to the Manchu custom of burning paper effigies and paper money as a part of the funeral services. Cf. Shirokogoroff 1935:214.

Beloved friend, *ara koro*
how short *ara koro*
was your life! *ara koro*
I heard *ara koro*
that a wise one was born. *ara koro*
I, withered old servant, *ara koro*
was happy. *ara koro*
Having heard talk *ara koro*
that you raised *ara koro* 20
a worthy prince, *ara koro*
I, stupid servant, *ara koro*
was hopeful. *ara koro*
Having heard *ara koro*
that you bore *ara koro*
a virtuous prince, *ara koro*
I, wicked servant, *ara koro*
relied on this. *ara koro*
Having heard of a prince *ara koro*
who was gifted, *ara koro*
I was wonder-struck. *ara koro*
How could this prince have died? *ara koro*

The people on the side were all brought to tears by the way he mourned to the very point of his own dying, striking the palm of his hand, angrily weeping and jumping up and down. When the official saw this he looked at the man sympathetically, took off the silk gown that he himself wore and gave it to the old man. The latter accepted the clothing, threw it over his shoulders and stood right at the head of the coffin. As he looked around the house he sighed 21 deeply and reproachfully said, "Rich sir, are you unblinkingly going to let go of Sergudai Fiyanggo and send him away? If there is a skilled shaman somewhere why don't you bring him here and have him bring the young master back to life!"

The official replied, "Where is there a good shaman? In this village of ours there are three or four shamans--all of the type who eat

by cheating people out of food. They are shamans who merely offer a little liquor, a chicken, and a few pastries or prepare some millet or grain. They not only don't revive a person; they don't even know the day and the time of his death.[7] I ask you, if there is a skilled shaman
22 somewhere that you, old man, know about, please give me some indication."

The old man replied, "Rich sir, how could you not know? There is a shaman[8] by the name of Teteke who lives on the banks of the Nisihai River[9] not far from here. This shaman has great power; she can revive the dead. Why don't you go to ask her? If she comes, even if there were ten Sergudais instead of one she would still be able to revive them! Go quickly and seek her!"

Having said this, he leisurely walked out of the main gate, sat on a five-colored cloud[10] and was lifted upwards. The gate guards saw this, and after they rushed into the house and reported it to the official, Baldu Bayan joyously
23 said, "Surely a god has come and instructed me!"

7. Among the Sibe a shaman must first prove his ability by correctly describing the circumstances of his patient's illness. If his answers concur with what really did happen according to the opinion of the sick person, he is acknowledged as competent [Krotkov n.d.:128].

8. Wherever the Manchu text has *saman* it has been translated simply as "shaman," whereas *saman gehe* (for standard Manchu *saman gege*) is translated either "shamaness" or "shaman, elder sister" depending upon the context.

9. There are two small tributaries of the Sungari River just south of Kirin that go by this name (Chinese *ni-shih-ha ho* 泥石哈河 and *ni-shih-ha ho* 泥使哈河 respectively). Cf. Fuchs 1943:122.

10. Probable Chinese and Buddhist influences. The image of an old man on a cloud suggests the common representation of an immortal in popular Taoism. The "five colors" (probably white, yellow, red, blue, and green) appear frequently in Buddhist iconography. Cf. Grünwedel 1970:138.

He then prostrated himself toward the empty space where the old man had stood. Mounting a quick-footed, gray, white-hooved gelding, he ordered his servants to follow. Setting out at a gallop, they reached the bank of the Nisihai River in no time. They saw a little hut on the east bank and Baldu Bayan noticed a young woman hanging out the clothes she had washed on a fence. He drew near and asked, "Elder sister, would you please tell me where the house of the Nišan shaman is?"

At this the woman smiled cheerfully and pointed, "She lives on the west bank."

The official then mounted his horse, and at full gallop he reached the place she had indicated. He saw that a person was standing inside the courtyard smoking tobacco. Hastily dismounting, he approached and asked, "Good sir, please 24
tell me which one is really the home of the Nišan shaman."

The man replied, "Why do you hurry about in such a frightened manner?"

"I inquire of you, sir, because I have an important and urgent affair. Please be so kind as to tell me."

Then the man said, "That woman who was hanging out her wash and whom you just questioned on the east bank is the very shaman! You have been tricked and deceived! When you make a request of that shaman, ask respectfully. She cannot be compared to other shamans. This one is very skilled at leading."

Baldu Bayan thanked the man, mounted his horse and again rode to the east bank. Getting down from his horse, he entered the house. He 25
noticed that an old, white-haired woman was sitting on the south oven-bed and a young woman stood smoking tobacco at the opening of the stove. The official thought, "The old woman who is sitting on the oven-bed is surely the shaman!"

He knelt down on the ground and was about

to make his request but the old woman said, "I am not the shaman. You, sir, have been misled. The one standing at the oven, my daughter-in-law, is the shaman."

Then Baldu Bayan got up and knelt before this woman and implored, "Shaman, elder sister, you have become famous and your name has spread abroad. Because you supersede twenty, even forty shamans, I have come to make a request of

26 you. Will you divine and indicate the circumstances of death? Although, elder sister, it is troublesome for you, what am I to do? Please be sympathetic and let me profit from your fame."

The woman smiled and said, "Mr. Bayan, I will not deceive you. I myself have learned shamanizing only recently, so I am afraid my divination of the circumstances of death will not be correct. Do not delay the matter! Seek other capable shamans and have them make the divition right away. Do not be careless!"

With tears flowing, Baldu Bayan knelt down and implored again and again. Following this the shaman said, "Because you came here first, I shall divine just once. If you were someone else, I surely would not divine."

Then she washed her face, set out the incense table, and threw the round *go* pieces into the water.[11] She placed a stool in the center of

27 the floor, grasped a tambourine in her right hand, wrapped the strap of the elm wood drumstick around her left hand, and, sitting on the stool and beating the tambourine, she began to entreat. Her beautiful voice calling out "*hobage*," her high voice repeating "*deyangku*," she implored in a chant, and the spirit permeated her body. Baldu Bayan knelt down on the ground and listened. The Nišan shaman began to mutter, and the words she muttered indicated this:

11. Presumably a method of divination.

Eikule yekule Man of this Baldu clan,
Eikule yekule (born in) the year of the dragon,
Eikule yekule listen!
Eikule yekule You, sir, have come
Eikule yekule to divine the circumstances of death.
Eikule yekule Listen clearly!
Eikule yekule If what I say is not so,
Eikule yekule say, 'It is not so,'
Eikule yekule If what I say is a lie,
Eikule yekule say, 'It is a lie.' 28
Eikule yekule A lying shaman deceives.
Eikule yekule Let me report to you:
Eikule yekule In your twenty-fifth year
Eikule yekule a boy
Eikule yekule was born.
Eikule yekule Having reached fifteen,
Eikule yekule he went to hunt
Eikule yekule on Heng Lang Mountain.
Eikule yekule On that mountain
Eikule yekule the evil spirit Kumuru
Eikule yekule seized and ate
Eikule yekule the soul
Eikule yekule of your son
Eikule yekule who himself
Eikule yekule got sick
Eikule yekule and died.
Eikule yekule Thereafter,
Eikule yekule there were no sons.
Eikule yekule In your fiftieth year
Eikule yekule I saw a boy 29
Eikule yekule and he was born.
Eikule yekule Because he was born
Eikule yekule at fifty years,
Eikule yekule you named him,
Eikule yekule saying, 'We will call you

Eikule yekule Sergudai Fiyanggo.'
Eikule yekule His worthy name has flourished.
Eikule yekule His great fame has gone forth.
Eikule yekule He reached his fifteenth year.
Eikule yekule As he was killing
Eikule yekule many beasts
Eikule yekule on the southern mountain
Eikule yekule Ilmun Han[12] heard this.
Eikule yekule He sent an evil spirit
Eikule yekule who seized his soul,
Eikule yekule taking it away.
Eikule yekule It will be difficult to revive him.
Eikule yekule I am concerned about reviving him.
Eikule yekule If what I say is so, say, 'It is so!"
30 *Eikule yekule* If what I say is not so, say, 'It is not so!'

Baldu Bayan, kneeling, said, "All that has been reported by the spirit, all that has been indicated by the narration, is correct."

The shaman grasped a stick of incense, raised it up, and revived. Then she put away the tambourine and drumstick. Baldu Bayan kowtowed again and again, and crying, said, "All that you have mercifully divined, shaman, is truly so. Because of this, please be so kind as to trouble yourself and in my humble home reanimate the dog-like existence of my son. Could I possibly forget the gods when you cause him to come back to life? Since I myself have sought you out, will I turn my back on recompense?"

After he said this, the Nišan shaman inquired, "In your home, I surmise there is

12. The Lord of the Underworld who acts as the judge of the dead [Shirokogoroff 1935:129].

probably a dog that was born on the same day as your son, and there is also a three-year-old rooster and various types of bean paste. Is this not so?" 31

Baldu Bayan answered, "Truly, what you have divined is correct. You are a wonderful, divine shaman! Now I would like to move your large implements for shamanizing; I would like to put your heavy implements on my shoulders. I implore you to please revive the young life of my son."

The Nišan shaman laughingly said, "How will I, a small and weak shaman, be able to accomplish this? You will spend your property and silver in vain and you will quickly exhaust your money to no benefit. Seek other capable shamans! As for me, I am a shaman who has just learned and who still has not acquired the fundamentals. A shaman who has learned only recently has not yet acquired official status. What do I know?"

32 Baldu Bayan knelt down on the ground. Bowing and crying bitterly he implored, "Shaman, elder sister, if you bring my son back to life, I will repay your kindness by giving you one-half of my gold, silver, silks, geldings, cows, and sheep."

After he said this the Nišan shaman had no alternative but to say, "Mr. Bayan, stand up! Let me go and vainly try to divine once. If I bring about good fortune, don't rejoice. If I am brought to failure, don't be disappointed. Please heed these words clearly!"

Rejoicing, Baldu Bayan stood up, and stuffing a pipe full of tobacco he thanked her, went out of the gate, and mounted his horse. As he approached his home he called Ahalji and Bahalji and said, "Quickly prepare a sedan chair, a wagon, and horses, and get the shaman."

33 Immediately Ahalji and Bahalji made preparations by completely and evenly hitching up the

wagons; then they took a group of servants and rode away to meet the shaman. In a short time they reached the house of the Nišan shaman on the bank of the Nisihai River where they met her. After greeting her they loaded the cabinets of spirit placings,[13] dividing these among three wagons. The shaman sat on the sedan chair, and with eight men carrying her as quickly as if they were flying, they reached the official's home in an instant. Baldu Bayan met her and conducted her into the house. He arranged the cabinets of spirit placings in the middle of the large oven-bed, washed his face, lit incense, and prostrated himself three times. Next the shaman washed her face and prepared some food. After she had finished eating she wiped her face with a damp towel and got her tambourine ready. She struck her tambourine and drum, praying in a murmur to the spirit; however, the three or four village shamans who struck their tambourines and accompanied her were so out of harmony that the Nišan shaman said, "If it is as discordant as this, how will I travel to the underworld?"

34

The official answered, "In our village there really are no capable people. If the shaman previously had a chief assistant who followed, tell me and I will have the servants go for him."

The Nišan shaman said, "There is seventy-year-old Nari Fiyanggo who lives in my village. This man will follow perfectly; he is well acquainted with the drum and chant. If this man comes, truly I will not worry. He has been filial and obedient."

At this the official immediately had Ahalji ride one horse, lead another, and quickly go to

13. A spirit placing is an object used as a "receptacle" or "locus" for physically "embodying" a spirit. Among the Tungus, placings are usually made of wood and tend to be anthropomorphic [Shirokogoroff 1935:190-97].

fetch Nari Fiyanggo. In a short time they got back and dismounted. Baldu Bayan met them, and as they were coming into the house the Nišan shaman saw them and laughingly said, "Noble sir, you who will give strength to the spirits, have you come? Virtuous Mr. Nari Fiyanggo, brother and assistant who will provide help for the gods, listen! Help me, your elder sister, by harmonizing beautifully with the tune. According to that which was established of old, I confidently entrust the tambourine and drum to you, brother and assistant. If you are unable, I will beat your thighs with a dampened, leather-covered drumstick. If you do not harmonize with the chanting and murmuring, I will beat your buttocks with a wet drumstick made of cherry wood!" 35

After she said this, Nari Fiyanggo laughed and replied, "Powerful, strange Nišan shaman, I, your younger brother, know this. I do not require a lot of instruction!"

He sat down on the oven-bed, prepared tea and food, and after finishing this he immediately harmonized, striking the drum. 36

Then the Nišan shaman tied the shaman's garments, bells, and skirts onto her body and put the nine-bird cap on her head. Her tall, slender body waved like a trembling willow, imitating the tune *Yang cun*;[14] it shook with her loud voice and rose up with her high voice. The soft tune winding, her subtle voice accompanying, she beseeched in a murmur:

> *Hoge yage* Please come, escaping
> *Hoge yage* from the stone pit!
> *Hoge yage* Please descend quickly!
> *Hoge yage*

As she spoke the shaman became disoriented

14. *Yang cun* (Chinese *yang-ch'un* 陽春) is the name of an ancient Chinese musical composition [Morohashi 1955-60:11:993].

and the spirit entered, permeating her fully. Suddenly, gritting her teeth, she began to mumble:

Hoge yage Lead assistant
Hoge yage standing to the side,
Hoge yage great assistant
Hoge yage standing next to me,
Hoge yage submissive assistant
37 *Hoge yage* standing near,
Hoge yage clever assistant
Hoge yage standing nearby,
Hoge yage having opened your thin ears,
Hoge yage listen!
Hoge yage Having closed your thick ears,
Hoge yage Listen!
Hoge yage Having fastened the rooster[15]
Hoge yage to my head,
Hoge yage make ready!
Hoge yage Having tied to my foot
Hoge yage the striped dog,[16]
Hoge yage make ready!
Hoge yage Place at my side
Hoge yage one hundred lumps
Hoge yage of old bean paste.[17]
Hoge yage Having wrapped one hundred bundles

15. The significance of the rooster in shamanizing is mentioned in passing by Krotkov (n.d.:132) in connection with a ceremony performed in order to bring back the wandering soul of one who has suffered soul loss: "In order to catch the soul, the shaman takes a rooster with him . . . and sets out to the fields at night."

16. In his description of burial preparations among the Tungus, Shirokogoroff [1935:210] notes that animals, especially dogs, must be kept away from the corpse, since dogs are believed to carry the soul into the lower world.

17. Shirokogoroff [1935:200]: "Generally, the Tungus and Manchus give the spirits those kinds and forms of food which they themselves appreciate unless there are special kinds and forms preferred by the spirits."

Hoge yage of coarse paper,
Hoge yage make ready!

Hoge yage I am going to pursue a soul
Hoge yage into a dark place.
Hoge yage I surmise that I will go
Hoge yage to the land of the dead.
Hoge yage I am going to fetch a life
Hoge yage in an evil place.
Hoge yage I am going to raise
Hoge yage a fallen soul.

Hoge yage Trusted assistant, 38
Hoge yage take charge of leading me.
Hoge yage Truly try hard
Hoge yage to revive me when I come back.
Hoge yage Throw water
Hoge yage around my nose:
Hoge yage twenty measures.
Hoge yage Pour water
Hoge yage around my face:
Hoge yage forty buckets.
Hoge yage

Having uttered this, she was thrown down and immediately her appearance began to change. Then the assistant, Nari Fiyanggo, approached her and had her lie down. He arranged the bells and skirt, tied up the rooster and the dog, and lined up the bean paste and paper. He seated himself next to the shaman and seized the drum; then he began to mutter, using the drumstick to 39 lead and conduct the spirits.

Cinggelji inggelji The candle
Cinggelji inggelji having been darkened,
Cinggelji inggelji tonight
Cinggelji inggelji for the sake of the soul
Cinggelji inggelji of Sergudai Fiyanggo
Cinggelji inggelji of the Bayara clan,

Cinggelji inggelji she has made a kowtow.
Cinggelji inggelji She is pursuing a soul
Cinggelji inggelji to a dark place.
Cinggelji inggelji She goes to fetch a life
Cinggelji inggelji in an evil place.
Cinggelji inggelji She is bringing support
Cinggelji inggelji for a dead soul.
Cinggelji inggelji As one powerful in regard to ghosts,
Cinggelji inggelji as one experienced with evil phantoms,
Cinggelji inggelji she is famous
Cinggelji inggelji throughout the world.
Cinggelji inggelji She is renowned
Cinggelji inggelji in all lands!
Cinggelji inggelji

40 After he said this, the Nišan shaman led the rooster and dog, put the bean paste and paper on her shoulders, and accompanied by all the spirits, she proceeded toward the land of the dead to seek Ilmun Han. As she went, the beast-spirits ran, the bird-spirits flew, and the serpents slithered. Traveling like a whirlwind she arrived at the bank of a river. Around her she noticed no place to cross; she saw neither ferry nor boat. While she was worriedly looking around, a man was traveling along the opposite bank by punting a boat. The Nišan shaman saw him and called out:

Hobage yebage Lame sir!
Hobage yebage Ferryman!
Hobage yebage Listen and take us!
Hobage yebage Having opened your thin ears,
41 *Hobage yebage* listen!

Hobage yebage Having closed your thick ears,
Hobage yebage please listen!
Hobage yebage Ugly Rogue,[18]
Hobage yebage won't you listen and remember?
Hobage yebage If the offerings are good
Hobage yebage you will become honored.
Hobage yebage If the offerings are good
Hobage yebage you will advance.
Hobage yebage Having acted as a lord,
Hobage yebage you will become virtuous.

Hobage yebage I am going to meet with the family of my father.
Hobage yebage I am going to rest with the family of my mother.
Hobage yebage I am going adorned
Hobage yebage to the house of my maternal grandfather.
Hobage yebage I proceed in dance
Hobage yebage to the place of my maternal grandmother.
Hobage yebage I go proudly
Hobage yebage to the home of my aunt (mother's younger sister).
Hobage yebage I go to fetch a life
Hobage yebage to the home of my uncle (father's younger brother). 42

Hobage yebage If you take me across
Hobage yebage I will give you bean paste.
Hobage yebage If you take me across quickly

18. The function of the Ugly Rogue is remarkably similar to that of Charon, the ferryman of the Greek underworld who carries the souls of the dead across the River Styx.

Hobage yebage I will give you paper.
Hobage yebage You will not take me to no avail;
Hobage yebage I will give you a fee.
Hobage yebage If you really take me across
Hobage yebage I will give you goods.
Hobage yebage If you take me across quickly
Hobage yebage I will present you
Hobage yebage with strong liquor.
Hobage yebage I go to redeem a life
Hobage yebage in an evil place.
Hobage yebage I go to pursue a soul
Hobage yebage in a dark place.
Hobage yebage

When the lame rogue heard this, rowing half a boat with half an oar he reached the opposite bank. The Nišan shaman saw that he had one eye, 43 a crooked nose, a shriveled ear, a bald head, a crippled foot, and deformed hands. He came near and said, "So you are the shamaness. If it were any other person I surely would not take him across, but since I have heard and am acquainted with your fame, and since the fate that has brought forth your name at this time is in order, it is impossible for me not to ferry you across."

After he said this, the Nišan shaman got into the boat. The lame rogue punted with his pole and rowed with his oar and they crossed to the other side. Afterwards she thanked him and said, "Take three lumps of bean paste and three bundles of paper and keep this as a small insignificant token." She also asked, "Hasn't anyone else gone across this ferry?"

44 The lame rogue replied, "No one else at all has crossed except for Monggoldai Nakcu, relative of the Lord of the Underworld, who passed taking the soul of Sergudai Fiyanggo, son of Baldu Bayan."

The Nišan shaman thanked him and then set off. Proceeding, she soon reached the bank of the Red River. When she looked around there was no boat to ferry her across and she did not even see the shadow of a person. Consequently there was nothing else to do; she began to murmur, beseeching the spirit:

Eikuli yekuli Great eagle
Eikuli yekuli circling the sky,
Eikuli yekuli silver wagtail
Eikuli yekuli circling the sea,
Eikuli yekuli malicious snake
Eikuli yekuli slithering along the river bank, 45
Eikuli yekuli eight pythons
Eikuli yekuli going along the Jan River--
Eikuli yekuli Young lord, I myself
Eikuli yekuli want to cross
Eikuli yekuli this river.
Eikuli yekuli All you spirits
Eikuli yekuli lifting me, ferry me across.
Eikuli yekuli Hurry!
Eikuli yekuli Reveal your power!
Eikuli yekuli

Then throwing her drum into the water the shaman herself stood on top of it, and like a whirlwind she crossed the river in an instant. She left a fee, three lumps of bean paste and three bundles of paper, for the lord of the river, and once again she set out. Since she traveled quickly she soon reached the main gate. She was about to go through the pass, but the two *hutu*[19] who were guarding the gate, Seletu and Senggitu, screeched, "What person dares to go through this pass? We guard this gate under order of Ilmun Han. Quickly report your business!" 46

The Nišan shaman said, "I am the Nišan shaman from the realm of the living. I am going to

19. A broad class of harmful spirits. "Seletu" and "Senggitu" are proper names derived from the common nouns *sele* "iron" and *senggi* "blood."

seek Monggoldai Nakcu in the realm of the dead."

The two *hutu* shouted, "If that is so, then according to the rule for entering the pass, one is allowed to pass through only after having left his name and a fee."

When they said this, the Nišan shaman gave them a name tally, three lumps of bean paste, and three bundles of paper. Only then did she go through. Traveling along, she reached a second gate, and as before she left her name and
47 a fee and then traveled through. She thereby reached the gate of Monggoldai Nakcu at the third pass. Her skirt bells shaking, the small bells ringing out, and she herself crying out "*Hoge yage*" in a beautiful voice, she said,

Monggoldai Nakcu,
Hoge yage quickly
Hoge yage come forth!
Hoge yage For what purpose
Hoge yage did you seize and bring here
Hoge yage one who did not have
Hoge yage a full length of life?
Hoge yage When it was not yet his time
Hoge yage you brought him here by force.
Hoge yage If you give him back
Hoge yage I will thank you generously.
Hoge yage If you give him free of charge
Hoge yage I shall thank you.
Hoge yage Halfway in life
Hoge yage you brought him here without reason.
Hoge yage You brought him here deceitfully!
Hoge yage What do you answer to this?

Hoge yage I will not take him away without paying;

Hoge yage I shall leave you a fee. 48
Hoge yage I will not take him away by deceit;
Hoge yage I shall leave goods.
Hoge yage If you give him to me
Hoge yage I will leave bean paste.
Hoge yage If you bring him out and give him to me
Hoge yage I will give you payment.
Hoge yage If you give him right away
Hoge yage I will pay my respects.
Hoge yage If you still do not give him
Hoge yage it will not be good.
Hoge yage The spirits in power will go in flight,
Hoge yage and entering your home
Hoge yage they will take him away!
Hoge yage

With skirt bells shaking, cap waving, and small bells ringing, the Nišan shaman was making her voice clang like metal. Just then Monggoldai Nakcu came out laughing and said, "Nišan shaman, listen carefully! It is true that I am the one who took away Sergudai Fiyanggo, son of Baldu Bayan. Of what concern is that to you? What have I stolen and brought here that is yours that you stand at my gate and bawl me out in a high, blundering voice?" 49

The Nišan shaman replied, "Although you have not stolen and brought here anything of mine, how could you bring an innocent child here, a person belonging to someone else, one who did not have a full length of life?"

Monggoldai Nakcu said, "That I brought him here was by command of our Ilmun Han. After we brought the child here, in order to test him we hung a gold coin on a high pole. We had him shoot an arrow at a hole in the coin, and he hit it each of the three times. Later, testing him again, we had him grapple with the blue wrestler

and the wrestler was consequently thrown. Next we had him grapple with the lion wrestler, and because the latter did not equal him, our Ilmun Han made Sergudai his son and is raising him
50 lovingly! Could it be possible to give him back to you?"

Listening to this speech the Nišan shaman became very angry and said to Monggoldai Nakcu, "If that is so, then it seems that this does not have anything to do with you. You after all are a good man. I have set out to seek Ilmun Han, and according to my own capability, I will either obtain or not obtain Sergudai Fiyanggo. If my power is great, then I will get him. If my power is insufficient, then I am finished. It does not have anything to do with you!"

Having said this, she set out to seek the city of the ruler, and in no time she arrived and saw that the gate was closed fast. Being unable to enter, the Nišan shaman looked around, but since the city walls had been built firm and solid she became angry and began to murmur:

51 *Kerani kerani* Great soaring bird
Kerani kerani nested
Kerani kerani on Eastern Mountain,
Kerani kerani sandalwood kingfisher
Kerani kerani on Cangling Mountain,
Kerani kerani oakwood badger
Kerani kerani resting
Kerani kerani on Mangga Mountain,
Kerani kerani nine snakes,
Kerani kerani eight pythons,
Kerani kerani small tiger,
Kerani kerani wolverine,
Kerani kerani resting
Kerani kerani in rocky lairs
Kerani kerani and iron passes,
Kerani kerani golden wagtail
Kerani kerani circling the mountain,
Kerani kerani silver wagtail

Kerani kerani circling the sea,
Kerani kerani flying hawk
Kerani kerani lead eagle,
Kerani kerani many-colored eagle,
Kerani kerani vultures of the earth, 52
Kerani kerani nine columns,
Kerani kerani twelve rows,
Kerani kerani flock of vultures--
Kerani kerani quickly
Kerani kerani enter the city by flying
Kerani kerani and bring him!
Kerani kerani With your talons
Kerani kerani grasping, bring him!
Kerani kerani With your claws
Kerani kerani seizing, bring him!
Kerani kerani Put him across your backs
Kerani kerani in a golden censer and bring him!
Kerani kerani Turn him over
Kerani kerani in a silver censer and bring him!
Kerani kerani By the strength of your shoulders
Kerani kerani lifting, bring him!
Kerani kerani

When she finished, all the spirits rose up in flight and became like clouds and fog.

As Sergudai Fiyanggo was playing with other children, tossing gold and silver anklebone dice, a great bird came down, seized him in his talons, and rising up, took him away. The other children saw this and were frightened. They ran into the house and reported to the ruler, their father, "Something bad has happened! A bird came, seized our brother Sergudai Fiyanggo, and took him away!" 53

When Ilmun Han heard this he became very angry. A *hutu* was dispatched who summoned Mong-goldai Nakcu and brought him to Ilmun Han.

Ilmun Han scolded him saying, "A great bird has seized and taken away Sergudai Fiyanggo whom you brought here. This had better not be of your doing! How could you possibly do this to me?"

As Ilmun Han said this Monggoldai calmly thought, "It is probably no one else but the Nišan shaman." Then he said, "Master, do not be angry. It is probably none other than the 54 Nišan shaman, who first appeared in the realm of the living and has since become well known in your great land, who has come and taken him away. I will go in pursuit now and try to find her. This shaman should not be compared to others!" Saying this, he set out at once in pursuit.

Meanwhile, the Nišan shaman was rejoicing greatly because she had obtained Sergudai Fiyanggo. She grasped his hand and was leading him back, but just as she was proceeding along the former route, Monggoldai, who was pursuing from behind, called out, "Shaman, elder sister, wait a moment! Let us talk a bit about right and wrong. Is it proper to take him away on the sly? I managed to bring him here with difficulty, spending a good deal of effort. Do you really intend to take Sergudai Fiyanggo away without payment, relying on your shamanism? Our Ilmun Han is angry and is blaming me. Now how can I answer? Shaman, elder sister, consider 55 this calmly: of course it is not in keeping with principles for you to take him away without even paying a fee!"

The Nišan shaman replied, "If you, Monggoldai, are merely asking me, I will still leave you a small fee. However, if you are acting forcibly, using your ruler as a prop, who fears you? We are faced with an important matter; let's settle it once and for all."

Saying this she gave him three lumps of bean paste and three handfuls of paper. Then

Monggoldai entreated again, "The fee you give is too small. Won't you increase it a bit more?"

The Nišan shaman gave him another portion but he again implored, "When I give this small fee to our ruler it will truly be of no avail. Alter all, how could he pardon my offense? What I request is that you, shaman, would leave me the rooster and the dog that you brought, and I will give them to Ilmun Han who would then pardon my offense, He has no dogs for hunting nor rooster to crow at night. Since our ruler would be pleased with these, in the first place your affair, shaman, would be settled, and in the second place he would pardon my offense." 56

The Nišan shaman replied, "That really would be advantageous for both sides. But only if you will grant Sergudai an increase in length of life will I leave you this dog and rooster and go away."

Monggoldai answered, "Shaman, elder sister, if you speak like this, then looking you in the eye I will add twenty years to his life span."

The shaman said, "Since you would take him at a time when his snivel is still not dry, it will be of no benefit." 57

"If that is the case, I will add thirty years of life."

"Since you would take him when his mind is not yet settled, it will be of no benefit."

"If that is the case, I will add forty years to his life."

"Since you would take him when he has not yet received honor and nobility, there would still be no benefit."

"If that is the case, I will add fifty years of life."

"Since you would take him when he is not yet wise and worthy, there will still be no benefit."

"If that is the case, I will add sixty years to his life."

"Since you would take him when he has not yet learned to use the bow and arrow, there would still be no benefit."

"If that is the case, I will add seventy years to his life."

"Since you would take him when he has not yet learned craftsmanship, there would still be no benefit."

"If that is the case, I will add eighty years to his life."

58 "Since you would take him when he does not yet understand the affairs of his age, there would still be no benefit."

"If that is the case, I will add ninety years to his life span. As for adding more, I cannot. From this time on, up to age sixty Sergudai will have no illness. Up to age one hundred he will not be frail. Let him raise nine children to gather around him. Let him see eight sons put a generation in motion. Until his hair turns white, his teeth turn yellow, his waist becomes bent, his eyes grow dim, and his feet begin to lag, let him urinate standing up and defecate squatting down."

At this the Nišan shaman thanked him and said, "If you grant sentiments such as this, I will give you both the rooster and the dog. Call the rooster by saying *Aši* and call the dog by saying *Ceo*."

59 Monggoldai Nakcu thanked her and was very happy. As he was leaving with the rooster and the dog, he thought, "Let me try calling them as a test."

When he released them and called out "*Aši, aši, ceo, ceo,*" both the rooster and the dog turned back and to his surprise went chasing after the Nišan shaman. Monggoldai was frightened and went running after them until he was out of breath. Gasping and panting he implored, "Shaman, elder sister, why do you play tricks? How is it that when I called your rooster and dog, they both turned around and went away? I beg of you, do not deceive me. If I do not take these two things back, this really will not work out. How will I be able to endure it when the ruler blames me?"

When he had implored again and again the Nišan shaman laughed and said, "I've joked enough. From now on remember well what I am going to tell you. Call the rooster by saying *Gu, gu,* and call the dog by saying *Eri, eri.*" 60

Then Monggoldai said, "Elder sister, you were only joking a bit, but I have broken out in a cold sweat."

When he called them according to what the shaman had said, both the rooster and the dog stayed close to Monggoldai and followed after him, wagging head and tail.

As the Nišan shaman was taking Sergudai by the hand and walking along leading him, she met her husband at the side of the road. She saw that he was boiling a cauldron of oil on a fire of sorghum stalks. Looking at his appearance she could see that he was angry. When he saw his wife he gnashed his teeth threateningly, and 61 hatefully said, "Fickle Nišan, instead of achieving the revival of all others, is there anything wrong with managing to revive me, your dear warm husband who was married to you from youth? I have especially boiled a cauldron of oil here and have been awaiting you. Quickly say whether you will bring me back to life or not. If you really won't revive me then I simply will not let you go on and this cauldron will immediately become your adversary!"

In reply the Nišan shaman entreated him:

Dear husband,
Hailambi šulembi listen quickly!
Hailambi šulembi Dear man,
Hailambi šulembi listen right here and now!
Hailambi šulembi Having opened your

thin ears,
Hailambi šulembi listen!
62 *Hailambi šulembi* Having closed your thick ears,
Hailambi šulembi please listen!
Hailambi šulembi The tendons and muscles of your body
Hailambi šulembi have broken apart.
Hailambi šulembi Being dead a long time,
Hailambi šulembi you have decayed.
Hailambi šulembi Your bones and flesh
Hailambi šulembi have all softened.
Hailambi šulembi How can I resurrect you?
Hailambi šulembi Dear husband,
Hailambi šulembi if you will consider me kindly,
Hailambi šulembi then please send me along, allowing me to pass.
Hailambi šulembi I will burn
Hailambi šulembi much paper money
Hailambi šulembi at your grave.
Hailambi šulembi I will offer in sacrifice
Hailambi šulembi a lot of millet and vegetables.
Hailambi šulembi I will care for and wait upon
Hailambi šulembi your mother.
Hailambi šulembi If you will consider this
63 *Hailambi šulembi* won't you spare my life?
Hailambi šulembi Having considered your old mother
Hailambi šulembi sympathetically,
Hailambi šulembi won't you let me pass?
Hailambi šulembi

When she finished begging like this her husband gnashed his teeth and hatefully said,

"Fickle, merciless Nišan shaman, wife, listen! During the time I was alive you despised me greatly, calling me wretched and closing your eyes to me. In your heart you clearly know this is so. You have acted according to your own whims, and whether you wait upon my old mother well or poorly is likewise according to your whims. Isn't this so in your eyes too? I wish to settle two grudges at once with you: the occasions of today and those of before. Decide quickly whether you will get into the cauldron of oil yourself or whether I will have to push you in!" 64

The shaman's face reddened at his speech and she angrily called out,

Dear husband, you listen!
Denikun denikun When you died
Denikun denikun what did you leave me?
Denikun denikun You left me
Denikun denikun your old mother
Denikun denikun in an impoverished household.
Denikun denikun I have respectfully nourished her.
Denikun denikun I have done my best to be filial to her.
Denikun denikun Husband,
Denikun denikun think and observe!
Denikun denikun I am
Denikun denikun a kind person.
Denikun denikun Having discovered
Denikun denikun your strong resolve
Denikun denikun I would like to give you
Denikun denikun a bit of a test. 65
Denikun denikun I will see if the strength of your corpse
Denikun denikun has been diminished.
Denikun denikun I am sending you
Denikun denikun to a suitable place.
Denikun denikun I beseech the spirits:

Denikun denikun Great crane
Denikun denikun circling above the forest,
Denikun denikun quickly
Denikun denikun seize in your claws
Denikun denikun my husband.
Denikun denikun Throw him for good
Denikun denikun into Fungtu City![20]
Denikun denikun Let him not take birth
Denikun denikun in a human body!
Denikun denikun

As she called out, a great crane took wing and immediately seized her husband in its claws and threw him into Fungtu City. The shaman saw this, and calling "*Deyangku*" in a high-pitched voice, she said,

66

Deyangku deyangku Without a husband
Deyangku deyangku I shall live happily.
Deyangku deyangku Without a man
Deyangku deyangku I shall live proudly.
Deyangku deyangku Among mother's relatives
Deyangku deyangku I shall live enjoyably.
Deyangku deyangku Facing the years
Deyangku deyangku I shall live happily.
Deyangku deyangku Without children
Deyangku deyangku I shall live on.
Deyangku deyangku Without a family
Deyangku deyangku I shall live lovingly.
Deyangku deyangku Pursuing my own youth
Deyangku deyangku I shall live as a guest.
Deyangku deyangku

20. This refers to the Chinese Feng-tu ch'eng 酆都城, the name of a city of the underworld that is most frequently mentioned in Taoist texts [Morohashi: 1955-60:11:345].

Chanting like this she led Sergudai Fiyanggo by the hand, now walking merrily as the breeze, now running quickly as a whirlwind. As she went along she saw a tower at the side of the road that had been built to be very majestic and beautiful, and five-colored clouds were piled around it. The Nišan shaman drew near and saw that two gods wearing gold armor and helmets were standing guard at the gate, holding iron clubs. She went closer and asked, "Sirs, please tell me what place this is and who lives inside." 67

To this the gods replied, "Omosi-mama,[21] who causes the leaves to unfurl and the roots to spread properly, lives in the tower."

The Nišan shaman said, "I would like to take advantage of my coming here and pay my respects to Omosi-mama. Is this in fact permissible?"

The gods at the gate responded, "It is permissible."

68 Thereupon the Nišan shaman thanked them with three handfuls of paper and three lumps of bean paste and went in. She reached the second gate and saw there were also two gods wearing

21. This spirit is believed to be in charge of the distribution of souls. According to Shirokogoroff [1935:52, 135], the Manchus conceive of the soul as being composed of three elements that are given to children by Omosi-mama: the "true soul," which may be compared with "consciousness" and which cannot leave the body without causing death; the "soul that precedes," which may temporarily leave the body during dreams and soul loss, and which returns to Omosi-mama after death so that she may give it to another child; the "external soul," which returns to Ilmun Han in the underworld after death, after which it may be reincarnated into another person or animal. Shirokogoroff also points out [1935:232] that Omosi-mama "is addressed with a sacrifice and prayer by the women in the cases of child delivery, sterility, also smallpox, chickenpox, measles and other similar diseases of children." This connection of Omosi-mama and smallpox can be noted in section 70 below.

armor and helmets who were standing guard. As the Nišan shaman was about to go in, they stopped her with a shout: "What kind of a person is entering this gate so heedlessly? Draw back at once! If you rush forward at all we will beat you!"

The Nišan shaman entreated them, "Great gods, do not be angry; I am not an evil spirit. I am the one known as the Nišan shaman from the land of the living. I only want to take advantage of my journey and meet and pay my respects to merciful Omosi-mama."

The two gods replied, "If you have such respectful intentions you may go in, but come out soon!"

At that the Nišan shaman again thanked them, left a fee and went in.

69 She reached the third gate where two gods were also standing guard. As before, she thanked them and went in. She saw that a five-colored vapor was shining within the tower and around the door a thick mist was billowing. There were also two women wearing garments of a five-colored pattern who were standing guard at the door. Their hair was dressed up high and in their hands they were holding gold censers. One of them was holding a silver dish and the other said with a smile, "It seems I recognize this woman. Aren't you the Nišan shaman who lives on the bank of the Nisihai River in the land of the living?"

The shaman was startled and responded, "Who are you? How could I have forgotten and not recognized you?"

The woman replied, "Why don't you remember 70 me? When I developed pox the year before last, Omosi-mama, calling me pure and good, brought me here and employs me at her side. We are neighbors of a single village. I was taken as wife by Nari Fiyanggo and within two days pox appeared and I died."

The Nišan shaman only then recognized her and joyfully exclaimed, "How could I have forgotten!"

Then the door was opened and she was ushered in. When she raised her head and looked up, she saw that an old woman whose hair was white as snow was sitting in the middle of the palace. Her eyes protruded, her mouth was large, her face long, her chin stuck out, and her teeth had become red--unpleasant to behold! On both sides more than ten women were standing. Some were carrying children on their backs, some were holding them in their arms, some were passing along yarn, and some were manufacturing small children. In addition, some were pushing the children along, some were putting them into bags, and others were loading them on their shoulders and carrying them away, going out through the eastern door. Everyone was very busy.

71

The Nišan shaman saw this and in astonishment knelt on the ground and bowed thrice three times--nine times in all. Omosi-mama asked "Who are you? Why don't I recognize you? You have come to this place recklessly!"

The Nišan shaman knelt and reported, "I, the small one, am known as the Nišan shaman who lives on the bank of the Nisihai River in the world of the living. Taking advantage of the road I have traveled to the underworld, I have come to visit and bow before the divine grandmother."

At this Omosi-mama said, "How could I have forgotten? When you were to be born, I became annoyed with you because you absolutely refused to go, and I placed a shaman's cap on your head, tied bells on your skirt, put a tambourine in your hand, and causing you to act as a shaman, I playfully brought you to life. It is proper that you have become famous. I myself ordained that you would someday come to this place, and

I have decided that after you are shown all the consequences of doing good and evil, you shall make this known to the world. It is determined
72 from the beginning who will come forth from here: shamans, learned ones, fathers and grandfathers, those who will become honored and revered, those who will do evil and create disorder, the rich, the poor, bandits, deceivers, Buddhist monks, Taoist priests, beggars, those who will drink, those who will gamble by cheating, those who will carouse with women--all good and evil. This is all fated!"

Then she told a subordinate, "Take the shaman and reveal some of the punishments, sorrows, and prohibitions."

Immediately a woman came, and urging the shaman forward she said, "Why don't you go for a stroll with me?"

The shaman followed and they set off together. She saw a forest that had grown to be very beautiful and luxuriant; the five colors were all present there in great abundance. When the shaman asked what this forest was, the woman
73 replied, "When Omosi-mama sees someone off to your world, she breaks off a willow branch from here and sends off those who have not eaten unclean, impure horses or cattle. Therefore this forest has grown well, and Omosi-mama's children's flowers are also good.[22] However, that forest over there has grown sparsely

22. Shirokogoroff [1935:236] refers to "flowering trees" also "blooming trees" and "beautiful trees" of the underworld, which are considered to be especially attractive to the *hutu*. When it is necessary to perform a ceremony in order to send away a particularly troublesome *hutu*, the specialist attracts and then "catches" the spirit with a representation of this tree --actually a willow branch decorated with white, red, blue, yellow, and green paper flowers instead of leaves. Shirokogoroff [1935:309] also notes the belief that "souls are living on beautiful trees"--a concept probably related to the above reference to Omosi-mama's children's flowers.

because willow branches there are used to send off to your world those who have eaten horses and cattle; consequently the children's flowers are bad and crimes and punishments are read out. This will all be shown and made clear to you."

Once again they set off. Inside a large building in the east a stone wheel was turning, and from within it all kinds of domestic animals, running beasts, flying birds, fish, insects, and various other living creatures in flocks and swarms were continuously running and flying out. The shaman saw this and asked about it, and her companion replied, "This is the place where we give life to all living creatures."

Again they went on and she saw the gates of a great city. Spirits and *hutu* were continuously walking through the gate. When she looked inside she saw the thick black fog of Fungtu City and she heard the loud weeping voices of the *hutu* within. There was also a village of wicked dogs. Encircling their prey, the dogs were tearing apart and eating human flesh. Inside a disorderly anteroom weeping voices crying out their sorrow and suffering shook the earth. Moreover, in the places of the bright-mirror mountain and the dark-mirror cliff the good and bad consequences were strictly separated. 74

Then the shaman saw an office. An official was sitting in the chamber judging all the souls. The ones hung up in the western wing were imprisoned criminals such as robbers and thieves. It was announced that those who had their necks put in cangues and were imprisoned in the eastern wing were those who had been unfilial to their parents or unfaithful to their husbands or wives. She also saw that those who had abused or beaten their parents were punished by being fried in cauldrons of oil. Pupils who had abused or shouted at their teachers were being punished by being tied to pillars while arrows were shot at them. Those who had bursts of temper against a husband or wife were being punished by being 75 cut up into small pieces. Taoist priests who had carried on illicit affairs with women, since they had polluted the scriptures, were being punished by being prodded with tridents. Those who had spilled rice and flour were being punished by being crushed between mortars and millstones. Those who had made false accusations and those who had broken agreements were being punished by being burned with iron chains that had been brought to a glowing redness.

Those who had made bribes when they were officials were being punished by having their flesh hooked. Those that had married two husbands were being punished by being violently cut up with saws. Those who had railed against their husbands were being punished by having their tongues sliced up. Those who had beaten down doors were being punished by having their
76 hands nailed down. Those who had stealthily eavesdropped were being punished by having their ears nailed to window frames. Those who had practiced theft and deception were being punished by being beaten with iron clubs. Women who had bathed in unclean streams and rivers and those who had washed away their filth on the day of the new moon or the day of the full moon were being punished by being made to drink muddy water.[23] Those who had looked askance at the aged were being punished by having their eyes hooked out. Those who had caroused with widows and young girls were being punished by being placed against pillars of fire and burned. Doctors who had wrongly administered drugs and who had caused death were being punished by being disemboweled. Women who had secretly and adulterously sought a husband were being punished by having their flesh hacked with an axe.

The shaman also saw a bridge of gold and

23. Very possibly related to the taboo observed among Tungus women: "Washing in lakes and rivers during menstruation is strictly prohibited" [Shirokogoroff 1929:260].

silver spanning a large lake. Those who walked on top of that bridge were all blessed people who had done good. Those who walked on a bridge made of bronze and steel were all people who had done evil. After *hutu* caused them to fall off the bridge by stabbing them with spears and grapplers, they were threatened by snakes and pythons. At the end of the bridge a vicious dog received them, and as it ate and drank the human flesh and blood people often called out, "I did not know evil!" 77

A bodhisattva sat at the side of the bridge, and holding a scripture in his hand, he made them all listen. The words of the book of precepts were such: "If you do evil, we will read aloud your punishments and transgressions in the land of the dead. If you do good, we will not call out any punishments. Persons of the highest class will occupy the position of Buddhas and rulers. Those of the second class will be reborn in palaces. Those of the third class will occupy positions as husbands of princesses or as grand preceptors. The fourth class will take positions as generals and high officials. The fifth class will become rich and noble. The sixth class will be reborn as common people and beggars. The seventh class will be reborn as donkeys, mules, horses, and cattle. The eighth class will be reborn as birds and beasts. The ninth class will be reborn transformed into turtles and fishes. The tenth class will be reborn transformed into worms, insects, and ants." 78

Reading this in a high-pitched voice, the bodhisattva made all listen to this advice.

After the Nišan shaman had finished seeing all the punishments she returned to the tower and bowed down to Omosi-mama, who said, "After you have arrived back in the world of the living, report this, making it understood to all men!"

Then bowing again, she departed. Leading Sergudai she traveled by way of the road she had come on previously and reached the bank of the

Red River. She gave a fee to the lord of the river, threw her tambourine into the river, and taking Sergudai she stood on top of it and crossed to the opposite side.

79 Traveling further, in a short time she reached the ferry of the lame rogue. Since she had passed by before he was familiar with her and said, "The shaman has arrived. You may truly be called a powerful shaman! You have obtained and brought back Sergudai Fiyanggo, son of Baldu Bayan: the achievement of your ability is not insignificant! Hereafter you will be even more famous!"

Then he urged her to get into the boat. The shaman took Sergudai, got into the boat and sat down, and the lame rogue rowed with half an oar so that they quickly crossed to the opposite bank. The shaman got out of the boat and thanked him by giving him a fee. Then, by traveling along the former road they soon reached the home of Baldu Bayan.

The chief assistant, Nari Fiyanggo, immediately poured twenty measures of water around her nose and forty buckets of water around her face. He grabbed some incense and sought to revive

80 her, and the words he murmured to awaken her were these:

> *Ke keku keku* This evening
> *Keku* we have turned out
> *Keku* the lamp and candle!
> *Keku* What was his reputation?
> *Keku* Whose reputation?
> *Keku* A hashūri of the clan,
> *Keku* truly a yashūri![24]
> *Keku* The Bayar clan
> *Keku* sprouted a leaf;
> *Keku* it grew a root.

24. This chant begins with a play upon words consisting of a parallelism in each couplet. The initial sound of the second word in the second line of each

Keku Sergudai Fiyanggo
Keku went hunting,
Keku became ill and died.
Keku For this reason,
Keku when three shamans discerned
Keku and four shamans considered,
Keku they said, 'Ilmun Han
Keku has taken his soul
Keku to the land of the dead.'

Keku Because of this
Keku she appeared foremost
Keku among the people
Keku who live on the bank
Keku of the Nisihai River.
Keku Her reputation came forth
Keku in the great land,
Keku so Baldu Bayan took in hand
Keku rue incense
Keku and went in pursuit
Keku beyond the mountain.

---

couplet is then changed to form a neologism that alliterates with the first word of that line. This is evident in the Manchu text:

keku ainaha algin
keku weinehe welgin
keku halai hashūri
keku yala yashūri

In the second line of the first couplet, *weinehe* stands for standard Manchu *weingge* "whose" and has probably been written in this fashion to form a syllable by syllable parallel with *ainaha* "what." *Welgin* is a neologism for "reputation" built from *algin*, the standard word for "reputation," which appears in the line before, transformed so that it alliterates with *weinehe*. In the second line of the second couplet *hashūri* is altered to *yashūri* to alliterate with *yala* "truly." However, the precise meaning of *hashūri* is problematic. It may relate to the Manchu word *hashū* "left" and refer to some aspect of the clan structure.

81 *Keku* When she took advantage of her reputation
Keku and tried to divine as an indication,
Keku because it was correct,
Keku beseeching, he brought her back.

Keku On this dark night
Keku she pursued a soul
Keku to a dark place.
Keku She has brought back a life
Keku from an evil place.
Keku She has returned.

Keku Lead eagle
Keku on the great branch
Keku of the immense willow
Keku accompanying,
Keku parti-colored eagle
Keku on the neighboring branch,
Keku golden wagtails
Keku circling the mountain,
Keku silver wagtails
Keku circling on high,
Keku small tiger,
Keku wolverine
Keku eight pythons,
Keku nine snakes,
Keku eight pairs of badgers
Keku from the sandalwood grove,
Keku ten pairs of badgers
Keku from the oakwood grove,
Keku may you come and revive her!
Keku May you bring her to life!
Keku Awake! Come to!

82 After he said this the Nišan shaman began to tremble. Suddenly she arose and started to murmur, and the words she murmured revealed what had happened:

Deyangku deyangku All people and assistants listen!
Deyangku deyangku Baldu Bayan, you yourself,
Deyangku deyangku listen item by item!
Deyangku deyangku Your son was brought back
Deyangku deyangku by being placed
Deyangku deyangku in a golden censer.
Deyangku deyangku He was brought back
Deyangku deyangku seized in its talons.
Deyangku deyangku I took away the treasure
Deyangku deyangku clasping him under my arm.

Deyangku deyangku I have put life
Deyangku deyangku into his dead body;
Deyangku deyangku I have infused a soul
Deyangku deyangku into his empty body.
Deyangku deyangku I beseeched Omosi-mama:
Kerani kerani 'Hereafter let him live
Kerani kerani without
Kerani kerani illness or weakness. 83
Kerani kerani Counting the good fortune
Kerani kerani of ninety years of life,
Kerani kerani let him raise nine children.'

Kerani kerani For Ilmun Han who took him away
Kerani kerani I left the rooster and the dog
Kerani kerani for his kindness.
Kerani kerani I left various payments.
Kerani kerani I met and bowed
Kerani kerani before Omosi-mama
Kerani kerani and also sought descendants

Kerani kerani for your son
Kerani kerani I will make it known to the world:
Kerani kerani When you serve Omosi-mama
Kerani kerani with respect and purity,
Kerani kerani Omosi-mama's flowers are good.
Kerani kerani Therefore do only good!
Kerani kerani If you do evil
Kerani kerani all the punishments are evident.
Kerani kerani I have seen each one with clarity.

84

Kerani kerani When my husband
Kerani kerani entreated me, saying
Kerani kerani 'Revive me!'
Kerani kerani my words were as follows:
Kerani kerani 'Your flesh and muscles have rotted;
Kerani kerani it would be difficult to resurrect you.'
Kerani kerani My husband became angry
Kerani kerani and was going to fry me to death
Kerani kerani in a cauldron of oil.
Kerani kerani Because of this
Kerani kerani a protective spirit of mine seized him
Kerani kerani and threw him
Kerani kerani into Fungtu City.
Kerani kerani For all eternity he will not take birth
Kerani kerani in a human body.

Kerani kerani Moreover, all the *hutu*
Deyangku deyangku were blocking the road
Deyangku deyangku continuously entreating

Deyangku deyangku 'Enliven our souls!'
Deyangku deyangku Their beseeching was pitiful
Deyangku deyangku but they were too numerous.
Deyangku deyangku I left many payments
Deyangku deyangku and all shared them. 85
Deyangku deyangku I have only come after divesting myself of all!
Deyangku deyangku

After saying this, she was thrown onto her back. The chief assistant used incense to make smoke swirl around her nose and only then did she awaken. Then, because the shaman herself fanned the soul into the empty body of Sergudai Fiyanggo, he suddenly came to. In a strong thick voice he said, "Please give me a bowl of water." After they brought it and gave it to him he drank it and said, "I've had a long sleep and have been dreaming for a while."

Then he rolled over and sat up, and the people of the house rejoiced. It was only when they reported the circumstances to Sergudai that he knew he had been dead. As Sergudai knelt before the Nišan shaman and thanked her, Baldu Bayan clapped his hands and laughed. He also said politely, "Truly you are a divine shaman. Lady, if you had not in your kindness brought my son back to life, the root would have been broken off!" 86

He then removed his cloak, put it on the shaman, and poured wine into cups of crystal and jade. He knelt down and offered it and the Nišan shaman accepted and drank it down to the dregs. Reciprocating his politeness she said, "If this has done nothing more than complete the good fortune of the official, then this is good fortune on both sides."

The official also poured a cup of wine and offered it to the chief assistant saying, "Please drink and quell your excessively sore throat a bit with our sour wine."

Nari Fiyanggo accepted the wine and while drinking it he said, "What was the trouble? From where I sat, as I didn't leave, it seems
87 there was no trouble at all. If I suffered, you, shaman, suffered much more. Since on this occasion you traveled to the land of the dead, you are probably extremely exhausted."

The shaman said with a smile, "Younger brother Fiyanggo, assistant, listen! There is a saying: 'If we consider a shaman equal to three parts, then unless there is a good assistant of seven parts, the shaman will not come back to life.'"

When everyone heard this they laughed loudly together.

Later the official Lo[25] called his two servants Ahalji and Bahalji and said, "Tell all the herdsmen of the cattle, horses, sheep, and pigs to divide each herd in half and make preparations. I would like to send this to the shaman in repayment for her kindness."

Then they prepared a feast, and they ate and drank so much that they all became very drunk.

After they removed the tables, they prepared the horses and wagons. The official collected one-half of his money, silver, and clothing
88 and put it in the wagons. For the assistant he gathered up a suit of clothes, one riding gelding, a saddle, a complete bridle, and two hundred taels of silver. The shaman and her assistant were then sent home with their things.

After this the Nišan shaman became very rich. She stopped the love affair she had been having with Nari Fiyanggo and settling down, began to live in an upright and proper manner, making a break with all strange, dissolute

25. "Lo" appears to be Baldu Bayan's Chinese surname.

matters. Since she had seen all the various types of punishments, her passion was diminished. Then she wrote down in outline all the sins and evils she had seen. It was like muddy water becoming all clean and clear by filtering. Men and women who hear this tale ought to examine these matters!

Later, the mother-in-law of the Nišan shaman had occasion to talk with the people of the village, and she heard that the shaman had seen her husband the time that she had traveled to 89 the underworld and that he had begged her, saying, "Enliven me! If you do not enliven me I will fry you to death in a cauldron of oil." At that time the Nišan shaman had relied upon her protective spirit, and after seizing her husband it had thrown him into Fungtu City. The shaman's mother-in-law became angry when she heard these reports. She summoned her daughter-in-law and asked exactly what had happened. The shaman's words were as follows:

"He said, 'Save me!' and I said, 'Your flesh has rotted and your muscles have fallen apart. It would be difficult to enliven you!' Then, when he said that he would fry your daughter-in-law to death in a cauldron of oil, it is true that my protective spirit seized him and threw him into Fungtu City."

The mother-in-law said, "If this is so, you have killed your husband a second time! Why could you not avoid the road where he sat? How difficult it is to think of this!"

Then she went to the capital city and made a complaint to the official censor. 90 By a summons from his office they brought the Nišan shaman there. When they took her deposition, because it was no different from the complaint presented by her mother-in-law, he wrote the report up as a memorial. When he sent this up to the ruler, indicating the general circumstances, the imperial decree said, "I am very angry. Hand this matter to the Board of Justice. Weighing her crime in the balance, proceed according to the law!"

The words that were sent up from the Board were these: "If we consider that the Nišan shaman did not conceal the matter which has been reported, then we must say that this woman has courage. But since we have received a deposition, she also can be made to pay with her life."

At this the Tai-tsung Emperor (r. 1626-43) sent down a decree: "Immediately gather the 91 shaman's cap, bells, tambourines, and implements, put them in a leather box, bind it tightly with steel rope and, as she got rid of her husband, get rid of them. Throw these things down the well that is in their village. Do not do anything but that which I command!"

When the decree came down, the official censor carried it out accordingly.

After this the son of the official Lo, Sergudai Fiyanggo, imitated his father's behavior by doing good, supporting the poor and providing help for those who had nothing. His sons and grandsons for generation after generation were officials, and they became very wealthy in money and silver.

Since this has become the book *Sain da deribun* (Good Origins) it has been taught to all. Despite this there are still evil teachings and goings on that are contrary to the great law. People in the future must not imitate them. Let us overcome and abstain from evil.

92 *What I, Dekdengge, instructor of Manchu at the Russian Oriental Institute (Vladivostok) request concerning these things is this: Mr. Grebenshchikov, I hope you will examine this text carefully from your point of view, and if there are any discrepancies would you please*

take a pen in your exalted hand and make additions and corrections. I have written these things for your information.

An Interpretation

In the preface Foucault's notion of the *episteme* was mentioned in connection with the varying epistemological premises and implications of anthropological research on shamanism. In a derived sense, Foucault's definition of this term can also suggest a way of integrating some final observations and conclusions regarding the translation presented here. A consideration of this tale's "field" and its "conditions of possibility" would necessarily involve an examination of both its textual and its contextual referents. Here the larger question--why was the tale so popular in this particular culture at this particular time--has a more specifically limited correlative: how was the story actually perceived in terms of plot and theme?

Before answering these questions, however, a few preliminary clarifications are in order. To be sure, the issues of text and context are so interrelated that it would be impossible to address one without simultaneously speaking to the other. Furthermore, the two terms themselves, which up to now have been used without any anthropological qualification, can also be amplified beyond the common acceptance of "text" as referring to a body of written language and "context" to a spatio-temporal setting. In the first case, James Boon provides a broad definition.

> I call a "text" any body of data in any sorts of units--sounds played, phones uttered, acts effected, colors applied, sentences writ, stars contemplated, geographical features surveyed, etc.--which smacks of systematization, *given an observer*. From such units systematically apprehended are derived music, speech, actions, paintings, paragraphs, constellations, maps, etc. respectively. Thus, in my usage a "text" could be composed of persons (categorically defined) interrelated in specific ways, just as well as of notes, words, graphics; the important point is that it be observed from without, with an inkling as to its systematic basis. Briefly then, "texts" are derived sensory systems [1973:10-11].

This extension of the notion of "text" beyond its usual referent--written language--correspondingly broadens the notion of "encoding," which can now refer as well to the process of analyzing any systematically perceived body of events, practices, activities, and so on. In the case of the Manchu shaman tale, then, the process of translation, which was initially carried out as a strictly linguistic operation, can now be undertaken in an analogous sense, this time in reference to other systematically organized bodies of data, whether the units of such be verbal or, as in the case of domains such as kinship and shamanism, largely nonverbal.

The second issue to require further clarification is the notion of context. Besides the general idea conveyed by this term, its specialized usage can also imply an additional referent in the specific case of folk literature: the totality of all the variants of a particular narrative. Here we encounter a problem with regard to the Manchu shaman tale. While we do have ethnographic evidence to indicate that this account was widely told and retold in its cultural setting, and while we also know that at least two other redactions of the tale exist in the archives of the Academy of Science of the U.S.S.R., we have at our disposal only one manuscript, that which was committed to writing at the beginning of this century by the Manchu, Dekdengge. In addition, we are here dealing with a culture that has ceased to exist. Thus we not only lack an "ensemble of variants," that is, a complete, systematized collection of the "compatibilities and incompatibilities" that characterize all the versions of the narrative (Lévi-Strauss 1960:25), in addition, we are also without any means of investigating living Manchu culture. While these factors would certainly impede our undertaking a complete structural analysis of the material, this lack of both contemporary data and an ensemble of variants should not rule out tentative attempts at interpretation, for as Lévi-Strauss himself points out, "other contexts exist, supplied by ritual, religious beliefs, superstitions, and also by positively-grounded knowledge" (ibid.). By interrelating as much data as we do have at our disposal, we can still delimit the general confines of the "universe of the tale," in this way indicating the direction a more thorough structural analysis would take if more contextual material were available.

Actually, it is the problem itself--the

lack of contemporary data on living Manchu culture--that points to a likely hypothesis regarding the tale's "conditions of possibility." Since the date of the known redactions corresponds roughly to the end of the Manchu era in China, and since both events occurred at a time when Manchu assimilation of Chinese ways was almost complete, is it not likely that the tale's temporal and thematic aspects are more than accidentally related? A definitive answer to this question must of course await more complete ethnographic documentation, but even at this initial stage of the investigation the hypothesis seems reasonable on this basis: throughout the long history of imperial China, its manner of assimilating neighboring "barbarian" groups did indeed provoke a situation where a non-Chinese cultural identity would have been a definite liability. In the case of the Manchus, however, one key factor served to remind these very successfully assimilated people of their native past: their system of social organization gave precedence to a belief in clan spirits, which in turn were directly involved in the practice of shamanism.

Shirokogoroff, who did his research at about the same time the Manchu dynasty was coming to an end, provides the documentation for this: "The Manchu clan is a group of relatives united by agnatic relationship, recognizing that they have a common ancestor and a group of spirits peculiar to these relatives" [1924:153].

In addition, he also connects these clan spirits with a belief system that served to affirm group identity via the related practice of shamanism.

> The ideology of the clan organization is closely bound up with the system of spirits adopted by the Manchus. The present Manchu

> shamanism is one of the elements forming the basis of the clan organization. Apart from shamanism the Manchu clan organization cannot exist, and being up to the present time unreplaced by any other philosophical and religious system, it protects the clan organization from final decomposition. Thus the clan organization has not only its genetic basis in shamanism, but shamanism also serves as a support for the social organization [ibid.:154].

While Shirokogoroff's conception of shamanism providing a genetic basis for clan organization seems questionable or at least unclear, his basic argument here is well supported by other data. Every Manchu clan had its own particular group of spirits, which were the specific ones addressed in shamanistic performances. These clan spirits included not only ancestor spirits, which Shirokogoroff considers to be a later Chinese addition, but also native Tungusic guardian spirits (often animals) that were of nonancestral origin. Other specifically Manchu beliefs and practices were not so deliberately passed down from generation to generation, for, according to Shirokogoroff, oral tradition at the time of Manchu rule over China was significantly weakened by the attitude that "the younger generations were depending on [for?] their success in [on?] the assimilation of the Chinese complex." However, there was this one exception: "the transmission of the tradition regarding clans and shamanism" (Shirokogoroff 1935:116).

The suggested link between this affirmation of cultural identity via the clan tradition and shamanism, and an at least unconscious negation of total sinification is further strengthened by the Manchus' own view regarding the first shaman. What is important here is not absolute historical verifiability, but rather that the Manchus *believed* this is what happened:

> During the Kin [Chin] Dynasty (1153-1234) there was a war between the Manchus and Chinese. The Chinese Emperor took hold of *cooha janggin* (the proper name of the first shaman, literally "soldiers' commander") and ordered him to be beheaded. So he was. But even beheaded the shaman did not fall down, and the Chinese Emperor called him *weceku* (guardian spirit) [Shirokogoroff 1935:276].

It would be simplistic to suggest that shamanism among the Manchus developed solely as a reaction against assimilation, for the intimate connection of shamanism with supernatural manipulation to bring about a desired effect can just as well reveal a central concern for functionalist utility in general. Nevertheless, the complex of beliefs and practices involved in shamanistic activity did serve to strengthen clan solidarity and affirm a particular group membership. In addition, this cause was further advanced by a related practice that was made possible by the invention of the Manchu alphabet circa 1600: the clan lists. These documents, specially kept by the clan chief, spelled out the precise terminological relationship of every member of the clan; a feat of considerable complexity in a culture where the full classificatory formula involved three or four agglutinated kinship terms. Special respect was accorded to these clan lists. They were considered secret documents that could not be shown to nonclan members, they were carefully recopied when they became old and worn, and the former copy was then ritually disposed of in "a great river"--usually either the Sungari or the Amur. Furthermore, the clan list had to be kept in some "good and pure place." Usually this meant keeping it with the spirit placings--the receptacles or loci for the spirits believed to inhabit such after being summoned there by the shaman (Shirokogoroff 1924:50,57). Here again the connection between shamanistic activity and Manchu self-affirmation is evident. Seen in terms of the mediation theme discussed previously, the data here already provide a preliminary confirmation of the initial hypothesis: it was not accidental that a tale based on shamanistic beliefs and tradition could find wide appeal at a time when an otherwise unbridgeable gap separated the native desire for self-affirmation from the unstoppable course of assimilation.

This rapprochement of mutually conflicting demands and pressures need not have been consciously recognized as such by the Manchus themselves. Nevertheless, their native beliefs regarding shamanistic power reflect a similar concern for mediation, represented in this case by the shaman's supposed ability to impose desired order on a situation of existential chaos. This latter concept, in the Manchu context, can be generally characterized as an incomprehensible threat to well-being. Sickness, untimely death, natural calamities, failures in hunting, and so forth were some of its more obvious manifestations, but beyond this it seems that these people's perception of their culture's impending disintegration might also have been felt as chaotic. In addition, the activity that was associated with this ideology made available a whole array of means and media that could serve to articulate chaotic states: a ritual, which could put temporal brackets around a particular performance and its object; a spoken or sung scenario, which could recreate and minutely describe the client's plight; a stylized appeal to more powerful forces, which were believed to be under the control of the shaman; an actively involved audience, who could collectively exteriorize their concern; and a general reaffirmation of shared beliefs and group consciousness. With all of these, the wild incomprehensibility of private terror could be controlled, bounded by known limits. Even if the shaman were to fail, the belief system would still have an explanation for this: more powerful spirits, who could now at least be identified. Thus chaos at its deepest level--uninterpretability--could not exist unmodified in this system; through shamanistic mediation, it could always be somewhat tamed and regulated.

Concomitantly, the concept of order that was associated with the shaman seems to have been fundamentally concerned with the latter's attempted restoration of a kind of wholeness or perfection. In accordance with native beliefs, the event of something going awry did not just represent an incidental, isolated loss or failure; rather, it suggested a fragmentation, a loss of vital contact with some kind of full potential, a disruption of cosmic oneness that would have otherwise allowed humanity to live out a noncorruptible existence (without sickness, death, or disintegration), perfectly integrated with nature (without problems in fulfilling biological needs). The shaman, of course, was not expected to bring about a total reordering of the cosmos, but because he was deemed able to travel back and forth between the realms of natural and supernatural problems and solutions, his existence could thus affirm the integrating belief that the chasm separating the chaos of the unknown and the senseless from the order of interpretability was indeed bridgeable.

Viewed from an anthropological perspective, shamanistic activity can be seen as a means of bringing together variously conceived oppositions--behavioral, cognitive, symbolic--that can be generally summarized in terms of order and chaos. While this characterization is not inaccurate with respect to Manchu shamanism of the late nineteenth and early twentieth centuries, it nonetheless ignores an important aspect of this specific case: at that time, Manchu culture was in the final stages of its existence, and the tension between an inevitable assimilation into the Chinese system and a fate-defying affirmation of its own unique patterns was also a part of the total picture.

A more complete way of considering all the facts in this case is suggested by Boon's broadly defined concept of text. Using this approach, the entire body of data here can be perceived in such a way that the whole system--the ritual, the actions, the clan lists, the spirit "placings," the six-volume native work on shamanism--can be read together as one integrated text. The key to its interpretation would then be provided by the one fact that could explain all the connections: the belief in clan spirits, which not only constituted the core of shamanistic activity, but which also supplied both natural and supernatural validation for an autonomous Manchu self-definition.

If cultural background can in this way be read as a text, then the shaman tale itself should logically be considered as a "text of a text," that is, a narrative composition whose elements are not just words, but words to the second power, simultaneously communicating on the level of everyday reality (the "text" of Manchu shamanistic activity) as well as the level of the deliberately constructed tale. Here too the same criteria can be used to find the key that would unlock the meaning of this text: it should permit a maximum understanding of the interconnections therein. The search for such a key can begin by considering the following abridged summary of the tale, paying particular attention to aspects that seem redundant and/or problematic.

The story begins with the birth of an only son, who dies suddenly at the age of fifteen while hunting on a mountain. The parents, "worried because they were without descendants," act in such a virtuous way that heaven rewards them with another son, but he too suddenly falls ill and dies on a hunting expedition. At the boy's funeral, an old hunchback appears and upbraids the boy's father for not summoning a shaman to bring the young heir back to life. The father finally succeeds in finding a properly qualified specialist, who turns out to be a young childless widow living with her mother-in-law. She agrees to go to the underworld to find the boy, but since the local shaman assistants are all incompetent, she insists on the presence and support of a seventy-year-old widower, with whom she obviously enjoys a close, joking relationship. The shamaness is successful in her journey to the underworld, but on her way back, she meets her dead husband, whom she adamantly refuses to bring back to life. Her explanatory chant to him contains a strong and surprising denial of all that a woman in Manchu culture should live for: husband, husband's clan, children, descendants. Before ending her underworld travels, she has one last adventure: a tour of its various hells, where "the consequences of doing good and evil" are clearly revealed to her. Coming out of her trance, the shamaness is greeted by the boy's grateful father, who is overjoyed to see his son alive again, because without him, "the root would have been broken off." After a celebratory feast, the shamaness, apparently affected by what she has seen in the underworld, ends her love affair with the old assistant and makes a break with "all strange dissolute matters." Taken to court by her mother-in-law for her refusal to revive her dead husband, her life is spared because of her honesty, but she is made to get rid of all her shamanizing equipment. The story ends by praising the upright behavior of the resurrected son, who goes on to become the long-lived begetter of "generation after generation" of successful officials.

Even this greatly abridged outline of the tale makes one aspect undeniably clear: the key to its interpretation must have something to do with the continuity of descent, crisscrossed by proper and improper social relationships. Thus the most likely domain to investigate at this point is the "text" of kinship.

Using Shirokogoroff's data, Lévi-Strauss has concluded that the latter, probably following the theoretical explanations of his Manchu informants, in effect described a system of restricted exchange in terms of generalized exchange (Lévi-Strauss 1969:377). He further employs a very apt label of double entendre by referring to the Manchu system as "the Chinese puzzle" in the theory of kinship systems.

> We are first faced with an often inextricable mixture of formulas of restricted and generalized exchange; secondly, perhaps with a transition from matrilineal descent to patrilineal descent; and finally, with the reshaping of all the factors of the primitive system under the influence of the Chinese system, the broad classificatory principles of which have been

> superimposed on the ancient forms. The result is a virtually unlimited number of kinship terms, formed for the most part by the combination and recombination of simpler terms [ibid.:379].

He then proceeds to illustrate this by describing the four Manchu categories of classificatory terms. First, the family group is divided into seven horizontal grades corresponding to generations: three ascending, Ego, and three descending. Then the group is likewise divided vertically into seven linear series of collateral relatives: the descendants of Ego's parents' brothers and sisters, of Ego's brothers and sisters, and of Ego. Thirdly, there are terms that seem to correspond to Chinese classifications: male, female, elder, younger, and distant.[1] Finally, a fourth group of simple or composite terms--some of which are direct borrowings from Chinese--serve as elementary terms. All of these four types of terms are combined freely, although most of the purely Manchu terms appear in the maternal clan (ibid.:380-83).

Lévi-Strauss pays special attention to the second class of terms, the lineal series, for he sees these as indicators of *segments* of different lines--a very likely indication that there was a former system--generalized exchange--that left behind several lineal categories that, as separate pieces, had to be fitted together into the consequent system of restricted exchange (ibid.:208). He further notes the Manchu practice of dividing each line into older and

1. The last term, *goro* (distant), apparently has no counterpart. Shirokogoroff [1924:180, n.xii] feels it might be a supplementary term related to the matrilineal clan and introduced after the Manchu kinship system changed from matrilineal to patrilineal.

younger branches--a classificatory distinction that suggests to him "a state of fluctuation between two marriage systems" (ibid.:386). His hypothesis for understanding this differential terminology for older and younger is as follows:

> If this distinction corresponded . . . to a formula of alternative marriage (in fact, if not necessarily legally), it would provide the means for the integral interpretation of the model of a society with exogamous moieties, each made up of several clans or lineages, united by a formula of asymmetrical marriage, but of different types according as the lineages are classed as "older" or "younger" [ibid.:271].

This is where the intersection of terms, relationships, attitudes, and behavior becomes especially significant in the Manchu data. As part of the spatial and sociological organization of the Manchu household, sleeping places on the *nahan* (the oven-bed platform mentioned in the story) are strictly prescribed according to an obligatory rule of alternation between members of the same class. Thus a whole system of social relations, particularly those connected with sexual privileges and prohibitions, can be associated with concepts of older, younger, adjacent, and nonadjacent. For example, it is absolutely prohibited for Ego to approach the wives of the men of his adjacent younger class (younger brother's wife), to speak with them, and even to touch the things that belong to them. On the other hand, there are no restrictions on Ego's relations and behavior toward the wives of the men of the older classes (older brother's wife; father's brother's wife): he may sleep beside them, and if they consent, he may have sexual relations with them (Shirokogoroff 1924:100).

This last point immediately catches our attention, for, if applicable to the situation of the shamaness and her assistant, a relationship that initially appeared illicit or at least puzzling, might still be in keeping with social norms after all. Going back to the complete tale, we find that this is indeed the case. Despite their differences in absolute ages, Teteke, the shamaness, consistently addresses Nari Fiyanggo, her assistant, as *deo*, which is the Manchu classificatory term for "younger brother." In turn, he and others in the story refer to her as *gege*, "elder sister," showing that the significant factor here is not an individual's absolute age, but rather his or her relative position in a lineage. But this is only the beginning, Further investigation of the tale in terms of kinship attitudes and expectations reveals an elaborate play of mirrors in which there is a constant crisscrossing of real and apparent, proper and improper.

The legitimacy of the first relationship, which initially appeared deviant, is balanced by the impropriety of other events, which at first glance might seem quite plausible. Seen in the light of Manchu expectations, Teteke's real transgression was not her sexual relationship with the old widower, but rather her strong affirmation of her clan of origin. According to Shirokogoroff (1924:142 n.1), "the woman, on her marriage, is considered as dead in her own clan," and "the widow's clan is the clan into which she was married." But Teteke, who could bargain with death to bring back life, was *not* dead to her clan; on the contrary, it was her *husband* whom she refused to reanimate, and both his and his mother's accusations against her suggest that even when he was alive she despised him and possibly even caused his death. This impression is further confirmed by the tone of her speech immediately after she has her husband thrown into Fungtu City: she renounces husband, family, and children, preferring instead to live "among mother's relatives." The same rejection of affinal clan and patrilineality appears in her chant to the lame boatman. She first upholds her own clan of origin ("I am going to meet with my father's family"), and then mentions four relatives on her mother's side (mother, maternal grandfather, maternal grandmother, mother's younger sister) before ending with another clan relative--father's younger brother.

It is precisely these reversals of proper attitudes and behavior that cause Teteke to be tried and sentenced in an imperial court. And yet this whole picture could be but a reverse image reflecting the values of an earlier time--now perhaps only mythically remembered--when matrilineality had not yet given way to patrilineal descent. While Shirokogoroff's positive statements on this last point (1924:48-49;70 n.1) cannot be definitively corroborated, we have other evidence to indicate that matrilineality has more than accidental importance in this scheme: given the confused mixture of variously combined indigenous and Chinese kinship nomenclature, the purely Manchu terms appear most often on the maternal side (ibid.:47,49).

The outlines of the key to the second text --the deliberately composed narrative--are beginning to take shape. An understanding of the Manchu kinship system, its expectations and prohibitions, certainly provides critical insights for an interpretation of the story's significance. But within this domain itself there is one issue that keeps appearing and reappearing in various guises, sometimes linked with the problems of the characters in the tale, other times linked with the circumstances of the first "text," that is, with the background of the Manchu system of shamanism that pervades the story. This issue, inherently a part of the time dimension, involves the two-headed problem of continuity and change.

On the level of the tale itself, this is undeniably the central theme of the whole work. The story opens with the sudden death of an only son, an event that, in the course of time, is followed by the heaven-sent birth of a second, who likewise meets an unnatural end, thus leaving his parents without descendants. The twists and turns of this theme, which moves predictably enough to its resolution, are intertwined with ominous variations that contrast the optimistic course of events--Sergudai Fiyanggo's return from the kingdom of the dead--with deliberate denials of lineage continuity: a young widow's choice of changeless death for her husband coupled with her repudiation of children, descendants, and affinal clan.

But this woman is also a shaman, a restorer of life (for nonrelatives), a specialist whose function is to mediate between the senseless chaos of an unnatural death and the negotiable acquisition of more life. She is mediator par excellence: an ambiguous creature with access to both natural and supernatural worlds. In both spheres she goes beyond, yet is ultimately subject to, the established social order. She plays tricks on both natural and supernatural characters (her initial deception of Baldu Bayan; her mischievous prank with the dog and the rooster), yet in the end she is expected to conform to group expectations (her trial and sentence), because she is, after all, subject to the laws of fate (as she was indeed reminded in Omosi-mama's realm).

Her equally ambiguous consort, Nari Fiyanggo, provides a less distinct, but clearly reversed image of the same type. While she is a young widow who leads the shamanizing performance and goes directly to the underworld, he is an old widower who follows, never going beyond the periphery of her supernatural journey. Yet their union, which the story's end seems to find improper in terms of mundane social conventions, was necessary in order for her to attain the supernatural realm. Once there, however, the same expectations of propriety do not seem to apply: when Nari Fiyanggo's former wife meets the shamaness in Omosi-mama's palace, she greets her with a smile.

Because of this mediating role of hers, Teteke also touches both sides of the problem of continuity and change. She succeeds in her mission to restore the grieving parents' only link with posterity, yet her goal is achieved only after her own status is changed and rechanged from earthbound inhabitant to supernatural visitor. By definitively choosing *not* to perpetuate herself or her clan down through time, she answers the natural concern for continuity with an un- or super- natural willingness to be obliterated by time, leaving behind her no links to the future. But perhaps this stand of hers against her own posterity is actually a protest against time that has already passed. Here again the text of the tale and the "text" of its historical background are composed of the same doubly significant elements. As has already been pointed out, Shirokogoroff believes that the original Manchu kinship system was matrilineal, a conclusion prompted by his study of the kinship terminology, where indeed the patrilineal group does show the most evidence of Chinese (i.e., later) influence. Now Teteke's striking repudiation of husband, family, and children occurs in a chant that also contains this significant couplet: "Among mother's relatives/ I shall live enjoyably." Consciously or unconsciously, the unknown author or authors of this tale could have been using this episode to make a plea for the old order, inserting here an almost subliminal remembrance of things past.

The ethnographic background behind this possibility is also doubly articulated in the tale and in historical reality. Even if the transition from matrilineal to patrilineal descent can remain no more than a hypothesis here, it is nevertheless undeniable that real changes have occured in the Manchu system, and the most important impetus for this has been Chinese influence. Thus a literary character who disregards social conventions by aligning herself with the "wrong" or "improper" kinship group could actually be an ironic device serving to affirm "real" propriety: the old order of the indigenous Manchu past.

While this possibility seems at first to be denied by the quintessentially Chinese ending of the tale, other considerations make it probable that the conclusion itself, with its moralizing tone, antishamanism attitude, and detailed references to the imperial bureaucracy, was a later addition. Neither of the other two versions of the tale collected by Grebenshchikov goes into any such detail; the first, only twenty-three pages long, ends with the shamaness's bargaining with Monggoldai Nakcu, and the second, fifty pages in all, consigns the episode of the destruction of her shamanizing equipment to a single sentence (Volkova 1961:8,10). An additional fact increases the likelihood that the ending of the redaction presented here was specially designed to appeal to sinified values: for the first time, Baldu Bayan is referred to by a Chinese surname.

The investigation of the "text" of kinship thus seems to have led to a conclusion that is but a variation of the first theme considered, Manchu shamanism. In that case, the belief in clan spirits was found to be the key that could unlock the interconnections of ideological belief and practice, additionally relating the whole complex to the temporal problem of assimilation and impending loss of cultural identity. The kinship "text" likewise contains this relentless theme, varying it by revealing in its terminology a backward look at an imperfectly remembered past. In both instances the inexorable course of time can be seen working on the elements of each system, pushing its own way forward toward an inevitable future, leaving behind bits and pieces of the past. Lévi-Strauss's metaphor is apt here: "The classification tends to be dismantled like a palace swept away upon the flood, whose parts, through the effect of currents and stagnant waters, obstacles and straits, come to be combined in a manner other than that intended by the architect" (1966:232). Finally, the tale itself, made up of these very bits and pieces of previous "texts," pays unconscious but eloquent homage to the same metaphor for the course of time: the ubiquitous image of water.

Like the shamaness herself, water, occurring in the form of a natural or supernatural river, clearly serves to mediate between these two realities. Teteke, the Nišan shamaness, lives on the east bank of the Nisihai River, which, thanks to her deceptive directions, Baldu Bayan must cross and recross in order to ask for her assistance. This function of demarcation between ordinary and extraordinary realms is more elaborately re-echoed in the geography of the underworld. With the help of the lame boatman the shamaness first crosses an unnamed river to get to the land of the dead; then, with the consent of the Lord of the River who allows her to travel on her tambourine, she crosses the Red River to arrive at the kingdom of Monggoldai Nakcu.[2] In both worlds, however, this clearly spatial boundary also delimits a transcendent temporal reality. Once Baldu Bayan has correctly crossed the river and entered her house, the shamaness is able to divine the critical events of his past, giving detailed and accurate account of the times of his sons' births and deaths. Likewise, having arrived at the center of the underworld, she is able to manipulate the future for her young charge, winning for the boy a guarantee of long life and posterity.

Water occurs in other forms in this tale, serving either as a bridge between important revelations and subsequent actions, or as a liminal association linking mundane activities with supernatural contexts. The numerous tears of the official, his wife, and the other earthly characters illustrate the first of these functions. The servants begin crying when they realize their young master is dead; this is followed by a realization of social propriety: "It is important that we take the corpse and begin our journey." Once the news of the boy's death reaches his home, weeping takes place in a progressively widening social milieu: parents, household servants, villagers; and again there is a reminder from the group that funeral preparations should be made. Then during the mother's tearful lament, "her tears flowed into a veritable river," and at this point the old hunchback, a precursor figure who introduces the shamaness, makes his entrance. Finally, Baldu

2. Shirokogoroff [1935:142] mentions a slightly different number and arrangement of rivers separating this world from the underworld: first, the Red River with the lame boatman, second, the Yellow River leading to Monggoldai Nakcu's realm, and third, the Black River beyond which Ilmun Khan reigns.

Bayan does not succeed in convincing Teteke to shamanize on behalf of his son until he beseeches her, first "with tears flowing," then "crying bitterly."

In addition to tears, other forms of water also serve to mark a character's transition from relative ignorance to greater knowledge. The pitiful old hunchback, who turns out to be the essential link between the dead boy's family and the powerful shamaness, is lifted to heaven on a five-colored cloud, a sign that reveals his supernatural status to the onlookers. Such clouds also occur in the underworld, where they serve to attract Teteke to Omosi-mama's palace. Finally, the shamaness's first encounter with the underworld place of retribution is preceded by her noticing the thick black fog of Fungtu City.

This transitional function of water, which in the above cases serves to connect an initially naïve understanding with a subsequent increase in knowledge, can alternatively be seen in another class of occurrences: mundane activities involving water. In such cases as the following, the ordinary nature of the action can also be transcended by association, with the water image becoming a symbol for purification and clarity: Teteke is hanging up clothes she has just washed when Baldu Bayan first sees her; she throws divination pieces into the water; she and the onlookers around her wash their faces before her shamanizing begins; she specifically asks to be brought back to a conscious state by having water poured around her nose and face; the reanimated boy asks for a bowl of water when he regains consciousness. Finally, a narrative aside at the story's end makes use of the same symbolic associations of this common, yet potentially transcendent substance: Teteke's written description of the retributions of the underworld is likened to "muddy water becoming clear and clean by filtering."

By following the thread of the investigation of kinship, in particular as it is related to the temporal problem of continuity and change, we have thus come to consider the polysemic metaphor of water. Heroclitus's river, always in flux; Lévi-Strauss's flood, dismantling palaces--such images are indeed inexorable. And yet a far gentler power, one recognized by baptisms and initiation ceremonies of all types, is also characteristic of water: by its possibility of mediating between the impure, profane, and the natural, on the one hand, and the pure, extraordinary, and the supernatural on the other, it can, shamanlike, bridge the gap between these two different planes of existence.

But water is but one element of this "text of texts," and its signifying possibilities, however rich, cannot account for all the other as yet unexplored articulations of the tale. The discovery of "a single structural scheme" existing and operating throughout all the contexts of Manchu culture would, in fact, satisfy Lévi-Strauss's goal in this respect, but as this is beyond the scope of the present work, let us more modestly conclude these observations and interpretations by indicating the direction a more complete structural analysis would take in this case.

Taking our cue from Lévi-Strauss's programmatic analysis of the story of Asdiwal (1967), we would begin by first distinguishing two different aspects of the shaman tale: its chronological sequences, which move lineally from beginning to end in the horizontal manner of a melodic line; and its contrapuntal schemes, which can be perceived as atemporal "chords" composed of logically related events. The first aspect, involving the progression from initial statement--the lack of descendants--to ultimate resolution--the promise of life and posterity--has already been considered. Let us now explore the second: the underlying principles of harmony found in this tale.

A scheme of the geographical data mentioned in the story would take into account the logical groupings of two different sets of oppositions: village and mountain, on the one hand, and south and east, on the other. The village is associated with propriety and the traditional social order. It is the villagers who persuade the grieving parents to make the requisite funeral preparations; likewise, at the end of the story it is only after Teteke's mother-in-law talks to "the people of the village" that she presses civil charges (in the capital *city*) against her daughter-in-law for the latter's behavior toward her husband. In contrast to this, the mountain is wild and chaotic. The deaths of both the older and younger sons of Baldu Bayan occur while they are hunting on a mountain; furthermore, Sergudai Fiyanggo's *indiscriminate* "killing of many beasts" is given as the reason for Ilmun Han's seizing his soul. Mountains are also recalled in the shamanizing songs: Teteke summons her guardian spirits who are "circling the mountain," and Baldu Bayan is mentioned as going to seek the shamaness "beyond the mountain."

This distinction is re-echoed in the relationship between the directional orientations south and east. Here south is associated with the human events that effectively change or manipulate the social order. Sergudai, whose death would have broken the continuity of his lineage, meets his end on the southern mountain. Teteke's mother-in-law, defender of proper familial behavior, is sitting on the south oven bed when we first meet her. On the other hand, east is the direction of otherworldly machinations, particularly those associated with the shamaness when she acts against ordinary social conventions. She lives on the east bank of the river, and we discover this in connection woth her deliberate deception of Baldu Bayan. Likewise, the crime for which she is tried--being improper in her relations with her husband--has its specified spatial correlative in the underworld: such souls are "imprisoned in the eastern wind." Finally, her primary guardian spirit, "the great bird" that assists her in her underworld schemes, nests on the eastern mountain.

A second scheme to be considered in this kind of analysis is provided by the cosmology, which in this story would include the layout of the underworld. In many respects the kingdom of the dead can be seen as a mirror image of the land of the living, and a complete structural analysis would take this fully into account, tracing the parallels and reversals and characterizing the underlying logic of the relationships. Here, however, we shall simply summarize the oppositions already discussed, associating "the upper world," "natural realm," and "proper social relations," on the one hand, and "the underworld," "supernatural realm," and "improper social relations" on the other.

The two final schemes to be characterized in this way would include data from the sociological and the economic settings. References to the kinship system in the shaman tale have already been considered in some detail, revealing an underlying tension between continuity and change, as expressed in the terms and attitudes corresponding to matrilineality and patrilineality, respectively. The economic scheme, then, would represent the last class of data to be examined. While a complete analysis would undoubtedly involve a much more thorough consideration of events connected with this sphere of activities, our tentative summary will simply characterize the basic opposition here as one between open and closed systems of exchange. In the first case, the two parties of an economic transaction are characteristically dependent on each other's reciprocity; such characters in the tale must bargain their way to a desired end. Teteke's entire mission is marked by this type of exchange: while she is paid for her services, she must herself pay others for theirs. Losses are overcome by gains and vice versa in these relationships, and this quality of mutual dependency and incompleteness is emphasized in the tale by specific references to fractions: the lame boatman's "half a boat with half an oar," the shamaness's reward of one-half of Baldu Bayan's possessions, the saying quoted by Teteke at the end of her journey: "If we consider a shaman equal to three parts, then unless there is a good assistant of seven parts, the shaman will not come back to life."

On the other hand, however, a closed system of exchange characterizes the underworld domain presided over by Omosi-mama. Here nothing new is ever added; nothing old totally disappears. In cyclic fashion life keeps appearing and then reappearing; as the overseer of this unending process, which is significantly symbolized by the turning stone wheel, Omosi-mama suffers no losses, but neither does she enjoy any profits. The reciprocal need that bargainers have for each other is thus contrasted by this autonomous being, who is ceaselessly self-sufficient in her own closed system.

To conclude this brief outline of the schematic aspects of the tale, let us integrate the above findings in the form of a simplified diagram, which also presents a reduced formula of the tale's sequential progression. The "melodic line," read horizontally, can be traced as the linear movement from initial to final state; the "harmonies," read vertically, are composed of the logically related schematic relationships.

Initial State →	*Final State*
[Death of sole heir]	[Life and posterity for lineage]
occurs correlated with:	*occurs correlated with:*
natural realm	supernatural realm
proper social relations	improper social relations
change in descent reckoning	continuity of descent reckoning
open, reciprocal system	closed, autonomous system

This provisional model, which is meant to be suggestive rather than conclusive, nonetheless permits further speculation, but first a few caveats are in order. We have repeatedly stated that this analysis can hardly be regarded as "complete," nor, in fact, is it ever likely to become such. Lacking both "the ensemble of the variants" and the possibility of actual contact with the tale's creators, we must therefore resign ourselves to the tentativeness of our conclusions. Despite all this, however, we have been supported in our efforts to understand this tale by a remarkable convergence of some very different anthropological perspectives. The concept of mediation, for example, has lent itself to a variety of approaches to the study of shamanism: behavioral, congnitive, symbolic, and structural. The last two concerns have been particularly important in the present study, but in all cases where this concept was applied--whether this be the tale, treated as an entity in itself; the cultural setting of Manchu shamanism, treated as a unique belief system; or the tale again, this time treated as a reflection of "a single structural scheme existing and operating in different contexts"--a focus on mediation was able to reveal key interconnections in the data.

It is this last point, with respect to the structural consideration, that still remains to be elaborated. The diagram on the previous page summarizes two groups of oppositions found in the tale: those connected with the initial state and those associated with the story's resolution. In all cases, the Nišan shamaness can link these oppositions, an event that can now be seen as logical as well as thematic. By her very ambiguity she is a mediator who bridges the gap between the two extremes. She has access to both natural and supernatural realms, yet she belongs fully to neither. She is tried for her transgressions, yet she transcends social norms; she recalls the past, yet secures a pledge for the future. Only in the last opposition--that between an open reciprocal system and a closed autonomous one--does her mediating ability falter. In that instance, bound by Omosi-mama's laws of predestination, she is only a temporary visitor to a self-sufficient realm, subject in the end to the course of her own destiny. But in this her plight is no different from that of the Manchu audiences who so appreciated this tale. For them as well it was the very last impasse that could not be resolved: "How can the native system remain viable if success comes from assimilating Chinese ways?"

The institution of shamanism could temporarily serve as a stopgap measure; it did, after all, actively draw on and proclaim that very tradition that was being depleted by the course of all other events. And the tale itself, composed of the bits and pieces of past times and present concerns, could still be perceived as somewhat fate-defying. But the ultimate form of propriety was change, not continuity. Only in the form of literature, where life is time-trapped and the present is always, could remembrances of the past survive into the future.

The Manchu Text: Transcription

In the transcribed text all serious textual problems such as nonstandard spellings and unusual lexical occurrences are noted only on their first appearance. Many of these problems have been correctly solved by Volkova (V) or Seong (S). In such cases their suggested reading is given in the footnote without comment. Where we wish to offer a solution different from that of V or S, our alternative follows theirs. Any note or statement not preceded by V or S is our own.

julgei ming gurun i forgon de. emu lolo sere. gašan bihe. ere tokso de tehe. emu baldu bayan sere. gebungge yuwan wai. boo banjirengge. umesi baktarakū bayan. takūrara ahasi morin lorin jergi toloho seme wajirakū. se dulin de emu jui banjifi. ujime tofohon se de isinafi emu inenggi boo ahasi sabe gamame. heng lang šan alin de abalame genefi. jugūn i andala nimeku baħafi bucehebi. tereci enen akū jalin facihiyašame. yuwan wai eigen sargan. damu sain be yabume. juktehen be niyeceme weileme. fucihi 1

de kesi baime hengkišeme. enduri de jalbirame.[1]
ayan hiyan de jafafi. ba bade hiyan dabume.
2 geli yadahūn urse de aisilame. umudu be wehiyeme. anggasi be aitubume. sain be yabufi ile-
tulere jakade. dergi abka gosifi susai se de
arkan seme emu jui ujifi. ambula urgunjeme gebu
be uthai susai sede banjiha. sergudai fiyanggo[2]
seme gebulefi. tana nicuke gese jilame. yasa
ci hokoburakū ujime. sunja sede isinafi tuwaci.
ere jui sure sektun.[3] gisun getuken ojoro jakade. uthai sefu solifi. boode bithe tacibume.
geli coohai erdemu gabtan niyamniyan be urebufi.
šun biya geri fari gabtara sirdan i gese hodon[4]
ofi. tofohon sede isinafi. gaitai emu inenggi
sergudai fiyanggo ini ama eme be acafi. baime
hendume. mini taciha gabtan niyamniyan be cen-
3 deme. emu mudan abalame tuciki sembi. ama i
gūnin de antaka be sarakū.[5] sehede ama hendume.
sini dergide emu ahūn bihe. tofohon sede heng
lang šan alin de abalame genefi beye dubehebi.
bi gūnici genere be nakareo sere jakade. sergudai fiyanggo hendume niyalma jalan de. haha
seme banjifi ai bade yaburakū. enteheme boo be
tuwakiyame bimbio. bucere banjire gemu meimeni
gajime jihe hesebun ci tucinderakū serede.
yuwan wai arga akū alime gaifi. hendume aika
abalame tuciki seci. ahalji bahalji sebe gamame
gene. ume inenggi goidare jebkešeme yabu. hahilame mari mini tatabure gūnin be. si ume
urgedere seme afabure be. sergudai fiyanggo je
4 seme jabufi. uthai ahalji sebe hūlafi afabume
hendume. muse cimari abalame tucimbi. niyalma.
morin. enggemu jergi be teksile. coohai agūra
beri niru jergi be belhe. cacari boo be. sejen

1. V,S: jalbarime
2. V,S: fiyanggū
3. V: sektu
4. V,S: hūdun
5. V: sarkū

de tebu. aculan[6] giyahūn kuri indahūn be saikan
i ulebufi belhe. sere jakade ahalji bahalji se
je seme uthai hahilame belheme genehe. jai inenggi sergudai fiyanggo ama eme de fakcara doroi
hengkilefi uthai sure[7] morin de yalufi ahalji
sebe dahalabufi aculan giyahūn be almime.[8] kuri
indahūn be kutuleme. geren ahasi se jebele dashūwan. beri niru unume. juleri amala faidan
meyen banjibume. sejen morin dahanduhai yaburengge. umesi kumungge wenjeshūn.[9] tokso sakda
asigan[10] urse gemu uce tucime tuwara akūngge   5
akū. gemu angga cibsime maktame saišambi. geren aba i urse morin be dabkiyame[11] yaburengge.
hūdun hahi ofi dartai endende[12] gebungge aba
abalara alin de isinafi. uthai cacari maikan be
cafi nere feteme mucen tebufi. budai faksi be
buda arabume werifi. sergudai fiyanggo geren
ahasi sabe gaime. ahalji bahalji sade afabume
aba saraki. alin šurdeme abalaki sefi uthai aba
sarafi. gabtarangge gabtambi. geli gadalarangge
gidalambi. giyahūn maktame indahūn cekuleme[13]
amcabumbi. gurgu gasha jergi be gabtaha. tome
gemu baharakū ningge akū. jing ni amtangga i
abalame yaburede. gaitai sergudai fiyanggo beye
gubci geceme. gaitai geli wenjeme. uju liyeli-   6
hun[14] ofi. nimekulere jakade. uthai ahalji
bahalji sebe hūlafi. musei aba faidan be hahilame bargiya mini beye icakū serede golofi hahilame aba be bargiyafi cacari de isinjifi beliyen[15] age be dosimbufi tuwa dabufi. tuwa de
fiyakūme nei tucibuki seci wenjere de taran wa-

6. S: anculan
7. V,S: suru
8. S: alamime
9. V,S: wenjehun
10. S: asihan
11. V,S: dabkime
12. S: andande
13. V: cukuleme
14. V,S: liyeliyehun
15. V,S: beile. *Beliyen* "foolish, doltish" cannot

liyame beye alime muterakū. ojoro jakade fiyakūme ojorakū ofi. ahasi sabe[16] alin moo be sacifi. kiyoo weilefi belin age be kiyoo de dedubufi. ahasi sa halanjame tukiyeme booi baru deyere gese yaburede. sergudai fiyanggo songgome hendume mini beye nimeku arbun be tuwaci ujen. ainahai boode isiname mutere ni bodoci
7 muterakū oho. ahalji bahalji suweni ahūn deo i dolo emke we inu okini. hahilame boode genefi mini ama eme de emu mejige benefi. mini gisun be ama eme de getuden i fonde[17] ularao. mini beye ama eme i jilame ujiha baili de karulame mutehekū. sakdasi i tanggū sede isinaha erinde hiyoošulame sinagalame fudeki seme majige gūniha bihe. we saha. abka gukubure jakade gūnihakū mini erin jalgan isinjire jakade. dere acame muterakū oho. yasa tuwahai aldasi bucembi. mini ama eme be ume fulu dababume nasame usara se. sakda beyebe ujirengge oyonggo. ere gemu gajime jihe hesebun i toktobuha ton kai. nasara songgoro be erilereo seme mini fonde getuken i ulam-
8 bureo seme hendufi. geli gisureki seci angga juwame muterakū. jain[18] jafabufi gisureme banjinarakū oho. sencike[19] tukiyeceme yasa hadanaha[20] ergen yadafi. ahalji bahalji geren ahasi se kiyoo be šurdeme ukufi songgoro jilgan de. alin holo gemu uradumbi.[21] amala ahalji songgoro be nakafi geren baru hendume. belin age emgeri bucehe. songgoro de inu weijubume muterakū oho.

---

be intended here. The spellings *beliyen* and *belin* alternate throughout the text.

16. It appears that *ahasi sa* "servants" is the subject of the verb *sacifi*. If so, it should not be followed by the object marker *be*.

17. S: funde

18. V,S: jayan

19. V,S: sencehe

20. S: hadahai. *Hadanaha* is a verb built from the form *hadambi* "to nail, to nail on" and the illative suffix *-na*. It is understood in the sense "to become fixed."

21. S: urandambi

giran be gaime jurarengge oyonggo bahalji sini beye geren be gaime belin age i giran be saikan hoššome[22] gajime elheo jio. mini beye juwan moringga niyalma be gamame neneme julesi genefi musei yuwan wai mafa de mejige alanafi boode belin age be. fudere jaka sabe belheme geneki seme alafi ahalji geren be gaime morin yalume. deyere gese feksime boo baru generengge hahi ofi. dartai andande boo i duka bade isinafi. morin ci ebufi boode dosifi. yuwan wai mafa de niyakūrafi damu den jilgan surume[23] songgombi. umai seme gisurerakū. yuwan wai mafa facihiyašame. tome[24] hendume ere aha si ainaha. abalame genefi ainu songgome amasi jihe. eici sini belin age ai oyonggo baita de simbe julesi takūraha ainu songgome gisurerakū seme siran i fonjire de ahalji jaburakū kemuni songgoro de yuwan wai mafa fancafi. tome hendume ere yeken akū[25] aha ainu alarakū damu songgombi. songgoro de baita wajimbio sehe manggi. songgoro be nakafi emgeri hengkilefi. hendume belin age jugūn de nimeme beye dubehe. mini beye neneme mejige benjime jihe. yuwan wai utulihe akū ai jaka dubehe seme fonjirede. ahalji jabume waka. belin age beye akū oho sere gisun be yuwan wai emgeri donjire jakade uju ninggude akjan guwehe gese haji jui seme surefi uthai oncohon tuheke de mama ekšeme jifi ahalji de fonjire jakade alame. belin age bucehe seme mejige alanjiha be donjifi. tuttu farame tuheke sehe manggi. mama

9

10

11

22. V equates *hoššome* with the verb *hošotolombi* "to prepare." Such an emendation is rather extreme. S understands the word as it stands. *Hoššombi* means "to coax" or "to ensnare"--*hūbišame eiterere be hoššombi sembi* [*Buleku*, 11:39b]. S translates the word as "treat respectfully" [p. 129], a meaning presumably derived from "to coax forward." Although S's interpretation is rather strained, it has been followed for lack of a better alternative.

23. V,S: sureme

24. V,S: toome

25. yeterakū

donjifi yasa julergide talkiyan gilmarjiha[26] gese menerefi. eme i jui seme emgeri hūlafi inu farame tob seme mafa i oilo hetu tuheke be takūrara urse golofi tukiyeme ilibufi. teni aituhabi. boo i gubci ere mejige be donjifi gemu songgocombi. ere songgoro jilgan de toksoi i[27] urse gemu isandufi gari miyari[28] seme ging[29] songgocoro namšan. bahalji songgome dosinjifi yuwan wai mafa de hengkilefi alame. belin age giran be gajime isinjiha yuwan wai eigen sargan toksoi urse sasa. dukai tule belin age i giran be okdome boode dosimbufi. besergen de sindafi. geren niyalma ukulefi[30] songgoro jilgan de abka

12 na gemu durgembi emu jergi songgoho manggi. geren niyalma tafulame hendume. bayan agu suweni mafa mama ainu utu[31] songgombi. emgeri bucehe songgoho seme weijure doro bio. giyan i giran de baitalara hobo jergi jaka be belheci acambi. sehe manggi yuwan wai eigen sargan teni nakafi hendume suweni gisun umesi giyan. udu tuttu bicibe yargiyan i gūnin dolo alime muterakū korsombi. mini haji sure jui emgeri bucehe kai. geli aibe hairambi. te geli ya emu juse de banjikini seme ten hethe werimbi. sefi ahalji bahalji sebe hūlafi afabume ere aha damu angga be juwafi songgombi. sini belin age de

13 nadan waliyara jaka. yarure morin. ku namun jergi be gemu belhe. ume hairara sefi ahalji bahalji se songgoro be nakafi afabuha gisun be dahame. belin age de yarure ilha boco alha akta morin juwan. tuwai boco jerde akta morin juwan. aisin boco sirga akta morin juwan. hūdun

26. V,S: gilmarjaha

27. Note the repetition of the genitive particle.

28. V,S: garl mari; gar miyar

29. V,S: jing. The author frequently writes g- for j- before the high front vowel. Cf. *jiramin* → *giramin*.

30. S understands *ukulefi* as it stands: "to turn down the brim of a hat." The author may have intended *ukumbi* "to gather around, to surround."

31. V,S: uttu

keri[32] akta morin juwan. šayan[33] boco suru akta morin juwan. behei boco sahaliyan akta morin juwan. gemu belhehe sehede yuwan wai afabume. gūsin morin de buktelii.[34] gecuhuri[35] etuku jergi be unubu. funcehe morin de jebele dashūwan jergi be alamibu. sure šeyen fulan akta morin de fulgiyan enggemu kadaragan[36] tuhebume aisin bolgiha[37] hadala jergi be yongkiyan tohofi yaru. geli adun i da sabe hūlafi. alame ihan adunci juwan gaju. honin adun ci ninju gaju. ulgiyan adun ci nadanju gaju. ere be gemu wafi belhe sehede. adun da. ahalji se je sefi jabumbime teisu teisu belheneme genehe. yuwan wai geli takūrara sargan jui aranju šaranju sebe hūlafi alame suweni juwe niyalma toksoi geren aisilara hehesi sebe gaime maise efen nadanju deren.[38] caise efen ninju deren. mudan efen susai deren. mere mudan dehi deren. arki juwan malu. niongniyaha juwan juru. niyehe orin juru. coko gūsin juru. sunja hacin tubihe guye[39] emte juwe deren. ere jergi be te uthai hahilame belheme yungkiyabu[40] tookabuci suwembe gemu tantambi. sehede. geren gemu je seme jabufi. meni meni fakcame belheneme genehe. goidaha akū geren niyalma gari miyari seme meyen meyen tukiyefi hūwa jalu faidame sindaha. barun[41] be tuwaci

14

15

32. S equates this word with *kuri* "spotted, dapple." The word *keire* is a more likely choice: "a dark-brown horse with a black tail and mane."

33. šanyan

34. S: buktulin

35. V: gecuheri

36. S: kandarhan

37. S: bulgiyaha. From the verb *bulgiyambi*: "to gild, to plate with gold."

38. V,S: dere

39. Both V and S transcribe as *buya* "small." However, the word appears to be written *guye* and is understood as a loan for Chinese *kuo* 菓 "fruit."

40. V,S: yongkiyabu

41. S equates this word with *baran* in the sense of "situation, circumstance." This meaning derives from the *Ch'ing-wen tsung-hui* 清文總彙 definition of *baran* as "military situation" [n.d.:103].

hada i gese den sabumbi. udu hacin yali alin i gese muhaliyahabi. arki mederi gese tebume sindahabi. tubihe efen deren sirandume faidahabi ku namun. aisin menggun hoošan jergi fiheme jalubume faidafi geren urse arki sisalafi[42] songgombi. dalbaci yuwan wai songgome hendume

ama i age ara.
susai sede ara.
ujihe ningge ara.
sergudai fiyanggo ara.
bi simbe sabuhade ara.
ambula urgunjehe ara.
16 ere utala morin ara.
ihan honin adun ara.
we salire ara.
age i ambalinggo[43] ara.
sure genggiyen ara.
ambula akdahabihe ara.
yalure akta ara.
ya age yalure ara.
aha nehu ara.
bihe seme ara.
ya ejin[44] takūrara ara.
aculan giyahūn ara.
bihe seme ara.
ya jui alire ara.
kuri indahūn ara.
bihe seme ara.
ya juse kutulere ara.

seme soksime songgoro de eme geli songgome hendume

eme i sure age ara.
eme mini ara.
enen juse ara.
jalin sain be ara.

However, Zakharov gives the secondary meaning "mass, large quantity" [1875:480], and this latter meaning has been followed here.

42. S relates to *sisambi* "to sprinkle."
43. V,S: ambalinggū
44. V,S: ejen

yabume baifi ara.
hūturi baime ara.
susai sede ara.
banjiha sure ara.
genggiyen age ara.
gala dacun ara.
gabsihiyan age ara.
giru saidan ara. 17
gicihiyan[45] age ara.
bithe hūlara ara.
jilgan haihūngga ara.
eme sure age ara.
te ya jui de ara.
nikeme banjimbi ara.
ahasi de gosingga ara.
ambulingga[46] age ara.
giru muru ara.
hocohūn[47] age ara.
fiyan banin ara.
pan an i gese ara.
saikan age ara.
eme giya[48] de ara.
šodome yabuci ara.
giyahūn adali ara.
eme jilgan be ara.
donjime baire ara.
holo de yabuci ara.
honggo[49] jilgan ara.
eniye hocohūn age ara.
eniye bi te ara.
ya emu age be ara.
tuwame bimbi ara.
gosime tembi ara.

45. V,S: gincihiyan
46. V,S: ambalinggū. Cf. fn. 43.
47. V,S: hocikon
48. V: giyan; S: giyai. The passage makes little sense if *eme* "mother" qualifies *giyai* "street." *Eme* should probably be understood as subject.
49. S: honggon

oncohon tuheci obinggi[50] tucime. umušhun[51]
18 tuheci silenggi eyeme. oforo niyaki be oton de waliyame. yasai muke be yala bira de eyebume songgoro de. dukai bade emu dara kumcuku[52] bucere hamika dara mehume yabure sakda mafa jifi hūlame hendume.

deyangku deyangku duka tuwakiyara
deyangku deyangku aguta sa donji
deyangku deyangku sini ejin de
deyangku deyangku genefi alarareo
deyangku deyangku duka tulergide
deyangku deyangku bucere sakda
deyangku deyangku jihebi sereo
deyangku deyangku majige acaki sereo
deyangku deyangku seme jihese[53]
deyangku deyangku majige gūnin
deyangku deyangku hoošan deijimbi.
deyangku deyangku

19 seme baire de duka tuwakiyaha niyalma dosifi baldu bayan de ulara jakade. yuwan wai hendume absi jilaka hūdun dosimbu belin age de waliyaha alin i gese yali efen be jekini. mederi gese arki be omikini sehe manggi duka tuwakiyaha niyalma sujume genefi tere sakda be hūlame dosimbufi. tere sakda dosime jidere de utala waliyara yali. efen arki jergi be tuwarakū. šuwe duleme genefi belin age i hobo hanci ilifi. gala hobo be sujame bethe fekuceme den jilgan i songgome hendume

age i haji ara koro
absi udu ara koro.
jalgan foholon ara koro.
sure banjiha ara koro.
seme donjiha ara koro
sungken[54] aha bi ara koro

50. S: obonggi
51. V,S: umušuhun
52. V,S: kumcuhun
53. S: jihe se. *Se* is the imperative form of *sembi* "to say."
54. V reads this word as *sunggiyen* "wise." S

urgunjehe bihe ara koro
mergen age be ara koro. 20
ujihe seme ara koro.
algin donjifi ara koro
mentuhun aha bi ara koro
erehe bihe ara koro
erdemu bisire ara koro
age be banjiha ara koro
seme donjifi ara koro
ehelinggo[55] aha bi ara koro
akdaha bihe ara koro
fengšen bisire ara koro
age be donjifi ara koro
ferguwehe bihe ara koro
age absi buceheni ara koro

galai falanggo[56] dume fancame songgome fekuceme bucetei songgoro be dalbai niyalmasa gemu yasai muke eyebumbi. yuwan wai sabufi šar seme gosime tuwafi. ini beyede etuhe suje sijihiyan[57] be sufi tere sakdade buhe manggi tere sakda etuku be alime gaifi beyede nerefi hobo ujui bade tob seme ilifi. emu jergi boo be šurdeme tuwafi ambarame emgeri sejilefi emu jergi jabcafi hendume bayan agu si yasa tuwahai sini jui sergudai fiyanggo be turibufi unggimbio. yaka bade mangga saman bici baime gafifi belin age be aitubureo. serede yuwan wai hendume aibide sain saman bi meni ere toksode emu ilan duin saman bi. gemu buda holtome jetere saman sa. damu majige arki. emu coko. heni efen jergi dobonggo[58] dobome ira buda belheme wecere saman sa kai. niyalma be weijubure sere anggala ini beye hono ya inenggi 21

---

equates the word with *sungke*, the perfective of *sumbi* "to congeal, to mature." V's interpretation does not give the term a pejorative connotation, which would be parallel to the speaker's other self-deprecatory first person references.

55. S: ehelinggu

56. S: falanggū

57. S: sijigiyan

58. V,S: dobon; *dobonggo* is the nominalized form of *dobombi* "to offer."

22 ai erinde bucere be gemu sarkū. bairengge sakda mafa aika bade sara mangga saman bici majige jorime alame bureo sehede. mafa hendume bayan agu si adarame sarkū nio. ere baci goro akū nisihai birai dalin de tehe. teteke gebungge hehe saman bi. ere saman erdemu amba bucehe niyalma be aitubume mutembi. tere be ainu baihanarakū tere saman jici. sergudai fiyanggo sere anggala uthai juwan sergudai sehe seme inu weijubume mutembi kai. suwe hūdun baihaname gene. seme gisurefi elhe nuhan i yabume amba duka be tucime genefi sunja boco tugi de tefi mukdehebe duka tuwakiyara niyalma sabufi hahilame boode dosifi yuwan wai de alaha manggi. baldu bayan urgunjeme hendume urunakū enduri jifi. minde jorime

23 taciburengge seme uthai untuhun baru hengkilefi ekšeme bethe sefere[59] sarala[60] akta morin yalufi. booi aha be dahalabufi. feksime goidahakū nisihai birai dalin de isinafi tuwaci dergi dubede emu ajige hetu boo bi. baldu bayan tuwaci tulergide emu se asihan gehe[61] jurhun[62] de oboho etuku be lakiyame walgiyambi. baldu bayan hanci genefi baime fonjime gehe nišan saman i boo ya bade tehebi. minde alame bureo serede tere hehe injeršeme[63] jorime wargi dubede tehebi sere gisun de yuwan wai morin yalume feksime isinafi tuwaci hūwa i dolo emu niyalma dambagu omime

59. S: seberi. Intervocalic *-b-* and *-f-* frequently alternate within this text.

60. S: sarla

61. S: gege

62. V: jorho; S: jerguwen. V. apparently understands *jorho* as a shortened form of *jorho fodoho* "a type of willow tree." S's interpretation is superior. Frequently in this text the vowel of one syllable will assimilate to the vowel of an adjacent syllable. Here *-e-* → *-u-* under influence of the *-u-* in the following syllable.

63. S: ijaršambi. The verb in the text may be a composite form arising from the author's confusion of the verb *ijaršambi* "to smile cheerfully" with the family of verbs related to *injembi* "to laugh."

ilihabi. ebuho sabuho[64] morin ci ebufi hanci 24
genefi baime sain agu wako.[65] nišan saman i boo
yala ya emke inu. bairengge tondo i alame bureo
serede tere niyalma hendume si ainu gelehe goloho
durun i ekšembi. yuwan wai hendume minde oyonggo ekšere baita bifi age de fonjime dacilambi.
gosici minde alame bureo tere niyalma uthai hendume si teni dergide fonjiha etuku silgiyafi
walgiyara tere hehe uthai saman inu. agu taša-
rabume holtobuha kai. tere saman be baire de
saikan i gingguleme baisu. gūwa saman de duibuleci ojorakū ere saman umesi dahabume kutulere
de amuran sefi. baldu bayan tere niyalma de baniha bufi morin yalufi dahūme feksime dergi dubede isinjifi. morin ci ebufi boode dosifi 25
tuwaci julergi nahan de emu funiyehe šaraka
sakda mama tehebi. jun i angga bade emu se asigan[66] hehe dambagu be gocime ilihabi. yuwan wai
gūnici ere nahan de tehe sakda mama jiduji saman
dere seme nada[67] niyakūrafi baire de sakda mama
hendume bi saman waka agu si tašarabuhabi. jun
bade ilihangge mini urun. saman inu serede
baldu bayan uthai ilifi ere gehe de niyakūrafi
baime hendume. saman gehe amba algin algikabi
gebu gūtubume tucikebi. orin saman i oilori.
dehi saman deleri turgunde. bairengge han julhun[68] 26

64. ebuhu sabuhū
65. S: wakao
66. S: asihan
67. nade
68. V suggests that this is the name of a disease, while S equates *julhun* with *julgen* "good fortune." In view of the alternation of velars *-g-* and *-h-* and the assimilation of vowels (see fn. 62), which occur throughout the text, S's interpretation is phonologically possible. However, if we follow S, *han* "king" becomes a problem. Shirokogoroff gives a spirit *naijulan* who "helps the shaman to find the cause of disease" [1935:174]. This is exactly what takes place in the passage above. Consequently, *han julhun* (=*han julan*?) "king spirit *julan*" may be an alternate name of *nai julan* "spirit *julan* of the earth."

be tuwabume jorimbureo[69] seme baime jihe gehe jobombi seme ainara šar seme gosifi algin be gaime bureo serede tere hehe injeršeme hendume bayan agu be bi holtorakū. mini beye ice tacifi goidaha akū de han julhun tuwarengge tondo akū ayoo ume baita be tookabure gūwa erdemungge saman sabe baifi erdeken i tuwabuna ume heoledere serede baldu bayan yasai muke eyebume. hengkišeme dahūn dabtan i baire jakade. saman hendume tuktan jihebe dahame. emu mudan tuwambureo gūwa niyalma oho bici ainaha seme tuwarakū bihe sefi dere yasa obufi.[70] hiyan dere faidafi.
27 muheliyen tonio be muke de maktafi. falan dulin de mulan teku be sindafi saman beye ice[71] galai yemcen[72] be jafafi hashū galai hailan moo gisun be halhifi[73] teku de teme yemcen be torgime geyeme[74] baime deribuhe hocohūn jilgan hobage be hūlame den jilgan deyangku be daginjime[75] yayame[76] baifi weceku be beyede singgebufi baldu bayan nade niyakūrafi donjimbi. nišan saman yayame deribuhe. jorime yayaha gisun.

eikule yekule ere baldu halai
eikule yekule muduri aniyangga
eikule yekule haha si donji
eikule yekule han be tuwabume
eikule yekule jihe age
eikule yekule getuken donji
eikule yekule waka seci
eikule yekule waka sebai
28 eikule yekule holo seci

69. S: joribureo
70. V,S: obofi
71. V,S: ici
72. V,S: imcin
73. V,S: halgifi
74. No suitable explanation of this word has been given. *Geyembi* means "to carve, to engrave," but such a meaning makes no sense here. From the context it would seem to mean something like "chant."
75. V,S: dahinjeme
76. V,S: yayadame, yayadaha

eikule yekule holo sebai
eikule yekule holo saman holtombi
eikule yekule suwende alarao
eikule yekule orin sunja sede
eikule yekule emu haha jui
eikule yekule ujihe bihe
eikule yekule tofohon se ofi
eikule yekule heng lang šan
eikule yekule alin de
eikule yekule kumuru[77] hutu
eikule yekule sini jui i
eikule yekule fainggo[78] be
eikule yekule jafame jefi
eikule yekule ini beye
eikule yekule nimeku bahafi
eikule yekule bucehe bi
eikule yekule tereci juse
eikule yekule ujihe akūbi
eikule yekule susai sede
eikule yekule emu haha jui 29
eikule yekule sabufi ujihebi
eikule yekule susai sede
eikule yekule banjiha ofi
eikule yekule gebube sergudai
eikule yekule fiyanggo sembi
eikule yekule seme gebulehebi
eikule yekule mergen gebu mukdeheci
eikule yekule amba gebu tucikebi
eikule yekule tofohon se ofi
eikule yekule julergi alin de
eikule yekule gurgu be ambula
eikule yekule waha turgunde
eikule yekule ilmun han donjifi
eikule yekule hutu be takūrafi
eikule yekule fainggo be jafafi
eikule yekule gamaha bi kai
eikule yekule weijubure de mangga
eikule yekule aitubure de jobombi

77. Probably the name of a spirit.
78. V,S: fayangga

30 eikule yekule inu seci inu se
eikule yekule waka seci waka se
eikule yekule

baldu bayan hengkišeme hendume wecen[79] i alahangge. geren julen i jorihangge gemu inu sehe manggi saman emge[80] hiyan be jafafi weshume[81] gelabufi yemcen gisun jergi be bargiyafi. baldu bayan dabtan i nade niyakūrafi songgome hendume saman gehe i gosime tuwahangge gemu yargiyan acanambi acanara be dahame gosici beyebe jobobume mini fosihūn[82] boode mini jui i indahūn gese ergen be aitubureo. ergen baha erinde enduri wecen be onggoroo dorombio. mini beye baiha be dahame basan[83] be cashūlara dorombio sehe manggi nišan
31 saman hendume sini boode ere jui i emu inenggi banjiha indahūn bi. geli ilan aniya amila coko. misun jergi amba muru bodoci bidere seme fonjirede baldu bayan hendume bisirengge yargiyan tuwahangge tondo kai. ferguwecuke enduri saman kai. te bi bahaci amba ahūra[84] be aššabumbi ujen ahūri be unume gamaki sembi. bairengge mini jui i ajigen ergen be aitubureo serede nišan saman injeme hendume ajige eberi saman ainaha icihiyame mutebure mekelen[85] bade ulin menggun fayambi tusa akū bade turgin[86] jiha wajimbi. gūwa mutere saman ṣabe baisu. bi serengge teni taciha saman tesu bahara unde. ice

79. V,S: weceku. *Wecen* alternates with *weceku* throughout this text in the meaning "protective spirit." The alternation of these two forms is noted by Shirokogoroff [1935:143].

80. V,S: emke
81. V: wesihume
82. V,S: fusihūn
83. V,S: basa
84. V,S: agūra
85. V,S: mekele

86. V,S: turigen. Such an interpretation is possible. *Turigen* means "rent money" and makes sense in the passage above. However, *turgen* "fast, quick" is also a possibility.

taciha saman ilban[87] bahara unde. aibe sambi
serede baldu bayan niyakūrafi hengkileme gosiho- 32
lome songgome bairengge saman gehe mini jui i
ergen be aitubuci aisin menggun alha gecuhuri
akta morin ihan honin jergi adun de dulin dendeme bufi baili de karulambi. sehe. manggi
nišan saman arga akū hendume bayan agu ilii[88] bi
bai emu mudan geneme tuwaki. jabsabuci inu ume
urgunjere ufarabuci inu ume usahara.[89] ere jergi
gisun be getuken i donjihao sehede. baldu bayan
ambula urgunjeme ubaliyame ilifi aname dambagu
tebume baniha bume wajifi uce tucime morin yalufi boo baru jime uthai ahalji bahalji sebe hūlafi hahilame giyoo[90] sejen morin jergi be belhefi
saman be ganareo serede uthai gemu teksin yung- 33
kiyan[91] tohome belhefi ahalji bahalji se geren
be gaime saman be okdonome yabume goidahakū
nisihai birai dalin i nišan saman i boode isinafi saman be acafi elhe baifi weceku guise jergi
be ilan sejen de dendeme tebufi saman giyoo de
tefi jakūn asihata tukiyeme deyere gese dartai
andande yuwan wai i boode isinjifi baldu bayan
okdome dosimbufi weceku guisebe amba nahan i
dulin de faidafi dere yasa obofi hiyan dabufi
ilan jergi hengkilefi amala saman dere obofi
buda belhefi jeme wajifi usihin fungku i dere
mafulafi[92] yemcen belhefi weceku de yayame baime
yemcen tungken forire de emu gašan de bisire 34
ilan duin saman sa dahalame yemcen forici gemu
mudande acanarakū ojoro jakade. nišan saman
hendume ere gese teksin akū oci absi hanilambi[93]

87. S reads this as it stands. V emends to *alban* "official capacity, duty, service." V's reading is preferable.

88. V: ili. Imperative of *ilimbi* "to stand up."

89. S: ushara

90. V,S: kiyoo

91. V: yongkiyan

92. S: mabulafi

93. V: kanilambi. S also relates it to the word *kani* "related, of the same class." It is difficult to make contextual sense from such an interpretation. Shirokogoroff lists a word *hanalambi*, which he defines

serede yuwan wai jabume meni emu tokso de yargiyan mutere niyalma akū oho. saman gehe de daci
dahalaha da jari bici alafi ganabuki sehede.
nišan saman hendume meni gašan de tehe nadanju
sede ujihe emu nara fiyanggo[94] bihebi. ere niyalma cingkai dahalara be dahame yemcen geyen
jergide gemu ureshūn gese ere niyalma jici
yargiyan i joborakū šašun[95] ijishūn bihe. serede yuwan wai uthai ahalji be emu morin yalubume
emu morin be kutuleme hahilame nara fiyanggo age
35 be ganabuha. goidahakū isinjifi morin ci ebufi
baldu bayan okdome boode dosime jiderede nišan
saman sabufi injeme hendume weceku de hūsun bure
wesihun agu jiheo endu[96] de aisilara erdemu age
nari fiyanggo deo. jari sini beye donji. gehe
minde saikan i mudan acabume aisila fe ilbaha[97]
be dahame yemcen tungken be deo jari de fita
akdahabi muterakū oci solho[98] ucihin[99] burihe.
sokū[100] gisen[101] ci wesihun i suksaha be tantambi. geyen yayan de acanarakū oci. uli moo i
usihin gisen ci ura be tantambi. sehe manggi
nari fiyanggo injeme hendume etenggi saman. de-
mungge nišan deo bi saha labdu taciburebe baibu-
36 rakū sefi nahan de tefi cai buda dagilame wajifi

---

as "to go to the dead world" [1935:308], a meaning that fits well in the passage above.

94. V,S: fiyanggū

95. Neither V or S give a suitable explanation of this word. It should be equated with the regular spelling *hiyoošun* "filial," which occurs in paragraph 75 below. It may have been misspelled under influence of the Chinese word *hsiao-shun* 孝順, upon which it was based; for the initial sound of the Chinese word had become a palatal fricative in the northern dialects.

96. S notes that this may be a shortened form of *onduri*.

97. V: ilibuha

98. V equates this with *solha* "a vessel for holding food," and S reads it as *solohi* "weasel." However, the word above is probably related to *sulhumbi* "damp" and is synonymous with the word *usihin*, which follows.

99. V,S: usihin

100. V,S: sukū

101. V,S: gisun

uthai tungken dume acabumbi. tereci nišan saman beyede ibagan i etuku. siša hosihan[102] be etume hūwaitafi. uyun cecike yekse be ujude hukšefi šunggayan beye sunggeljere fodoho i gese. uyaljame yang cun i mudan be alhūdame. amba jilgan i acinggiyame. den jilgan i dekenime.[103] haihūngga mudan hayaljame narhūn jilgan nadame[104] yayame baire gisun.

hoge yage wehei ukdun
hoge yage ukcame jidereo
hoge yage hahilame ebunjireo
hoge yage

serede saman hūlhidafi fikenci[105] fita singgeme weceku dosifi gaitai weihe saime yayame alame.

hoge yage dalbade iliha
hoge yage dalaha jari
hoge yage adame iliha
hoge yage amba jari
hoge yage hanci iliha

37

hoge yage haihūngga jari
hoge yage šurdeme iliha
hoge yage sure jari
hoge yage nekeliyen šan
hoge yage neifi donji
hoge yage giramin[106] šan
hoge yage gidafi donji
hoge yage amila coko be
hoge yage uju bade
hoge yage hūwaitafi belhe

102. V,S: hūsihan

103. S correctly suggests that this is a verb built up from *deken* "rather high."

104. V: adame; S: nandame. The latter intepretation is followed.

105. S gives two possible explanations of this word. It may be the ablative of *fike* "the upper part of the leg" or the ablative of *fisa* "the back." Our translation reflects the belief that this is the conditional-temporal converb of *fihembi* "to fill." Thus, the extra tooth transcribed above as *-n-* is the author's orthographic mistake.

106. V,S: jiramin

hoge yage kuri indahūn be
hoge yage bethe jakade
hoge yage siderefi belhe
hoge yage tanggū dalhan[107]
hoge yage fe misun be
hoge yage dalbade sinda
hoge yage tanggū sefere
hoge yage suseri hoošan be
hoge yage hosifi[108] belhe
hoge yage farhūn bade
hoge yage fainggo be farganambi
hoge yage bucehe gurun de
hoge yage buhime[109] genembi
38 hoge yage ehe bade
hoge yage ergen be ganambi
hoge yage tuheke fainggo be
hoge yage tunggiyeme yombi
hoge yage akdaha jari
hoge yage yarume gamareo
hoge yage yargiyan fede
hoge yage aitubume jidere de
hoge yage oforo šurdeme
hoge yage orin damjin[110]
hoge yage muke makta
hoge yage dere šurdeme
hoge yage dehi hunio
hoge yage muke hungkure[111]
hoge yage

seme alafi uthai fahabume gūwaliyame tuheke manggi jari nari fiyanggo okdome dedubufi siša hosihan jergi be dasatafi coko indahūn be hūwaitafi. misun hoošan jergi be faidame sindafi ini beye saman i adame tefi weceku fideme yarume
39 gamara gisun i nari fiyanggo yemcen be jafafi yayame deribuhe terei geyen

cinggelji inggelji dengjan ayan be

107. V,S: dalgan
108. V,S: hūsifi
109. S: buhiyeme
110. V,S: damjan
111. V,S: hungkere

cinggelji inggelji farhūn obufi
cinggelji inggelji ineku yamji de
cinggelji inggelji bayara halai
cinggelji inggelji sergudai fiyanggo
cinggelji inggelji fainggo jalin
cinggelji inggelji hungken[112] de hujufi
cinggelji inggelji farhūn bade
cinggelji inggelji fainggo be fargambi
cinggelji inggelji ehe bade
cinggelji inggelji ergen be ganambi
cinggelji inggelji tuheke fainggo be
cinggelji inggelji tunkiyeme[113] gajimbi
cinggelji inggelji hutu de hosungge[114]
cinggelji inggelji ibagan de icingga
cinggelji inggelji abkai fejergide
cinggelji inggelji algin bihe
cinggelji inggelji geren gurunde
cinggelji inggelji gebu bihe
cinggelji inggelji

sefi nišan saman coko indahūn be kutulefi misun hoošan be meiherefi geren weceku šurdeme dahalafi bucehe gurun i baru ilmun han be baime genere de gurgu wecen feksime. gasha wecen deyeme meihe jabjan muyaljime[115] edun su i gese yabume emu birai cikin dalin de isinjifi šurdeme tuwaci umai doore bakū[116] bime dokūn[117] weihu geli saburakū jing ni facihiyašame tuware namšan cargi bakcin dalin de emu niyalma be šurume yabumbi. nišan saman sabufi hūlame hendume 40

hobage yebage dogūn dobure[118]

112. *Hungken* is a unit of money and makes no sense in this context. Neither V or S propose a solution to this problem. The author most likely intended *hengkin* "a kowtow." This would go well with the verb *hujumbi* "to prostrate," which follows.

113. V,S: tukiyeme

114. S: hūsungge

115. S: probably a blend of *midaljambi* "to slither" and *uyaljambi* "to wind like a snake."

116. S: = ba akū

117. V,S: dogon

118. V: doobure

hobage yebage doholo[119] age
hobage yebage donjime gaisu
hobage yebage nekeliyen šan be
hobage yebage neifi dongi
41 hobage yebage giramin šan be
hobage yebage gidafi donjireo
hobage yebage arsun[120] laihi[121]
hobage yebage ejeme donjireo
hobage yebage wecen sain de
hobage yebage wesihun oho
hobage yebage jukten sain de
hobage yebage julesi oho
hobage yebage ejin ilifi
hobage yebage erdemungge oho
hobage yebage amai dancin[122] de
hobage yebage acame genembi
hobage yebage eniyei dancin de
hobage yebage ergeneme[123] yumbi[124]
hobage yebage goro mafa boode
hobage yebage goirame[125] genembi
hobage yebage goro mama bade
hobage yebage maksime yumbi
hobage yebage deheme boode
hobage yebage dekdešeme[126] genembi
42 hobage yebage ecike i boode
hobage yebage ergen be ganambi
hobage yebage mimbe doobuci
hobage yebage misun bumbi

119. V,S: doholon

120. V takes *arsun* as the proper name of the ferryman. However, as S notes, *arsun* may simply be a misspelling of *ersun* "ugly, repulsive."

121. V,S: laihūn

122. V interprets this word as *dacun* "decisive, resolute." S reads it as *dancan* "the wife's family." In this context S's interpretation is preferable.

123. V: ergenume; S: ergendume. Both of these words mean "rest."

124. yombi

125. S equates this to *goidambi* "to last for a long time." A superior reading, which would make it semantically parallel to the line below, is *goimarambi* "to adorn oneself."

126. V,S: dekderšembi

hobage yebage hūdun doobuci
hobage yebage hoošan bumbi
hobage yebage bai dooburakū
hobage yebage basan bumbi
hobage yebage unenggi doobuci
hobage yebage ulin bumbi
hobage yebage hahilame doobuci
hobage yebage hatan arki
hobage yebage alibume bumbi
hobage yebage ehe bade
hobage yebage ergen be jolinambi
hobage yebage farhūn bade
hobage yebage fainggo be farganambi
hobage yebage

serede doholo laihi donjifi hontoho cuwan be hontoho selbi i selbime bakcin ergi dalin de isinjifi nišan saman tuwaci yasa gakta[127] oforo waikū.[128] šan kemteku.[129] uju kalji.[130] bethe doholo. gala gaba.[131] hanci jifi hendume saman hehe nio aika gūwa niyalma oho biheci ainaha seme dooburakū bihe. gebu algin be donjime takame ofi giyan i ere mudan mergen gebu tucire hesebun giyan ofi. arga akū simbe doobumbi sefi nišan saman weihu de tafafi doholo laihi šurku[132] i šurume. selbi selbime cargi bakcin de boobuha manggi nišan saman baniha bume ere majige untuhun gūnin ilan dalhan misun. ilan sefere hoošan be gemu bargiyame werireo sefi. geli fonjime ere dogūn be yaka niyalma dome[133] genehe akū seme fonjihade doholo laihi alame   43 44

127. S: gakda

128. S: waiku. This word has a variant spelling *waihū*, and the spelling in the text above may be a blend of these two forms.

129. V: emte. V's explanation is too radical, and S offers no alternative. The spelling above may be a distortion of a word related to *kengcembi* "to collapse" (of soft things).

130. V,S: kalja

131. S: gafa

132. V,S: šuruku

133. V,S: doome, dooha

umai gūwa niyalma doho akū damu han niyaman monggoldai nakcu baldu bayan i haha jui sergudai fiyanggo faingo be gamame duleke. nišan saman baniha bume. uthai juraha. yabume goidahakū geli fulgiyan birai dalin de isinafi šurdeme tuwaci dokūn doobure jahūdai akū bime emu niyalma helmen be inu saburakū ofi arga akū weceku be baime yayame deribuhe

eikuli yekuli abka be šurdere
eikuli yekuli amba daimin[134]
eikuli yekuli mederi be šurdere
eikuli yekuli menggun inggalii[135]
eikuli yekuli bira cikin be šurdere
eikuli yekuli cecereku[136] meihe
45 eikuli yekuli jan bira be šurdere
eikuli yekuli jakūn da jabjan
eikuli yekuli ajige ejin mini beye
eikuli yekuli ere bira be
eikuli yekuli doombi[137] sembi
eikuli yekuli geren wecense
eikuli yekuli wehiyeme dooburo[138]
eikuli yekuli hūdun hasa
eikuli yekuli erdemu be tucibureo
eikuli yekuli

sefi yemcen be bira muke de maktafi saman i beye ninggude ilifi uthai edun su i gese dartai andande bira be doofi. bira ejin de ilan dalhan misun. ilan sefere hoošan basan werifi uthai jurame yaburengge hahi ofi uju furdan de isinjifi duleki
46 serede furdan tuwakiyaha seletu senggitu juwe hutu esukiyeme hendume ainaha niyalma gelhun akū ere furdan be dosiki sembi. be

134. V,S: damin
135. V: inggali
136. V,S: cecercuke
137. From the context of this passage, it would seem that the desiderative form of doombi was intended: *dooki sembi* "want to cross."
138. V,S: doobureo--the polite imperative of *doolumbi*.

ilmun han i hese be alifi ere furdan be tuwakiyambi. hūdun turgun be ula serede nišan saman hendume mini beye weihun gurun i nišan saman inu. bucehe gurun be monggoldai nakcu be baihanambi sehede juwe hutu esukiyeme tuttu oci furdan dosire kooli gebu. basan be werifi dosimbumbi sehede nišan saman gebu afahari ilan dalhan misun. ilan sefere hoošan be bufi teni duleme genehebi. yabume jai furdan de isinafi inu onggolo songkoi gebu basan jergi werifi duleme yabuhai ilaci furdan i monggoldai nakcu i duka bade isinafi siša lasihiyame.[139] honggo hoyome[140] hocohon jilgan i hoge hūlame 47

monggoldai nakcu
hoge yage hūdun hahi
hoge yage tucime jidereo
hoge yage ai jalin de
hoge yage sain i banjire
hoge yage jalgan akūngge
hoge yage jafafi gajiha
hoge yage erin unde
hoge yage ergeleme gajiha
hoge yage amasi buci
hoge yage ambula baniha
hoge yage bai buci
hoge yage baniha bumbi
hoge yage banjire aldasi
hoge yage balai gajiha
hoge yage eitereme gajiha
hoge yage aiseme jabumbio
hoge yage bai gamarakū
hoge yage basan bumbi

48

139. V,S: lasihime

140. S suggests that *hūyame* may be the verb intended by the author. The latter is defined in the lexical sources as "to cry (of eagles)." However, there is a tendency for the dictionaries, based as they are upon earlier Chinese sources, to be overly specific in defining Manchu terms. The verb may mean simply "to sound" and describe a number of different types of sounds, bells as well as the sound of eagles.

hoge yage holtome gamarakū
hoge yage hūda werimbi
hoge yage minde buci
hoge yage misun bumbi
hoge yage tucibufi buci
hoge yage turgin[141] bumbi
hoge yage doigonde buci
hoge yage dorolombi
hoge yage geli burakūci
hoge yage sain ba akū
hoge yage weceku hūsunde
hoge yage deyeme genembi
hoge yage boo de dosime
hoge yage ganame genembi
hoge yage

seme nišan saman siša lasihiyame yekse isihime honggo hoyodome[142] halang[143] sere jilgan be gu-
49 webure jakade monggoldai nakcu injeme tucifi hendume nišan saman getuken i donji bi baldu bayan i haha jui sergudai fiyanggo be gajihangge yargiyan sinde ai dalji bi sini booi ai jaka be hūlhafi gajiha seme mini duka bade ilifi den wakalan jilgan i dangsimbi serede. nišan saman hendume udu hacin i mini jaka be hūlafi gajihakū bicibe weri sain banjire jalgan akū niyalma be. sui akū jui be gajici ombio. monggoldai nakcu hendume meni ilmun han hese gajihangge. tere jui be gajifi. cendeme den siltan de aisin jiha lakiyafi jiha sangga be gabtabure jakade ilan da gemu gūwaihabi.[144] amala geli cendeme lamun buku i baru jafanabure[145] jakade buku be tuhebuhebi. geli arsulan[146] buku i baru jafanabuci inu hami-
50 rakū ofi meni ilmun han jui obufi jilame ujimbi

141. S: turigen
142. This word is built up from the verb we previously equated with *hūyambi*.
143. S: kalang
144. S: goihabi
145. S: jafunubure, jafunubuci
146. S: arsalan

kai. sinde amasi bure doro bio seme emu fiyelen gisun be nišan saman donjifi. ambula jili banjifi monggoldai nakcu i baru hendume tuttu oci sinde heni dalji akū dere. si emu sain niyalma biheni. mini ecehen[147] i ilmun han be baihanafi sergudai fiyanggo be bahara baharakū. ujude mini erdemu amba oci. uthai gajimbi. erdemu cinggiyan[148] oci uthai wajiha. sinde heni dalji akū sefi. han i hoton be baime geneme goidaha akū isinafi tuwaci duka be akdulame yaksihabi. nišan saman dosime muterakū šurdeme tuwafi hoton weilehe ningge akdun beki ofi ambula fancafi yayame deribuhe

kerani kerani dergi alin de 51
kerani kerani tomoho
kerani kerani dekdere gasha
kerani kerani cangling alin de
kerani kerani cakūra[149] moo canggisa[150]
kerani kerani mangkan alin de
kerani kerani tomoho
kerani kerani mangmoo[151] manggisa[152]
kerani kerani uyun da meihe
kerani kerani jakūn da jabjan
kerani kerani wehe ukdun
kerani kerani sele guwan[153] de
kerani kerani tomoho
kerani kerani taran[154] tasha

147. S: encehen

148. cinggiya

149. S: cakūran

150. S suggests that this is a spirit's proper name. The word is probably to be identified with *cunggaisa*, the plural of "kingfisher."

151. S: mangga moo

152. manggisu

153. S suggests that this word is to be identified with Chinese *kuan* 關 "pass." V translates the word as "cage," a reading that makes good contextual sense but is not justified by any Chinese word with such a reading. Another possibility is that the Chinese word intended was *k'uang* 礦 "mine."

154. S: targan

kerani kerani onioko[155] lefu
kerani kerani alin be šurdere
kerani kerani aisin inggali
kerani kerani mukden be šurdere
kerani kerani menggun inggali
kerani kerani deyere giyahūn
kerani kerani dalaha daimin
kerani kerani alaha[156] daimin
kerani kerani nai jule[157] se
52 kerani kerani uyun uri[158]
kerani kerani juwan juwe faidan
kerani kerani geren julese
kerani kerani hūdun hahi
kerani kerani deyeme hoton de
kerani kerani dosifi gajireo
kerani kerani wašiha[159] ci
kerani kerani wašihalame[160] gajireo
kerani kerani šoforo ci
kerani kerani šoforome gajireo
kerani kerani aisin hiyanglu[161] de
kerani kerani alamime tebufi gaju
kerani kerani menggun hiyanglu de
kerani kerani ungkufi[162] gaju
kerani kerani meiren i hūsun de

155. V,S: ongnika. Note that in the *Wu-t'i ch'ing-wen chien* 五體清文鑑, *ongnika* "wolverine" is listed with the different types of bears [1966:910].

156. S: alha. This word has been elongated by one syllable above in order to parallel *dalaha*.

157. S suggests that *jule* should be identified with *jolo* of the compound *ekcin jolo* "a very ugly person." However, the word is parallel to the names of various animals, and we would suggest that it should be equated with *yolo* "vulture."

158. *Uri* appears in the dictionaries as "a round straw container used for storing grain." However, its meaning in this context is problematic.

159. V,S: wasiha

160. V,S: wasihalame

161. This is to be identified with Chinese *hsiang-lu* 香鑪 "censer."

162. S: ungkefi

kerani kerani meihereme gajireo
kerani kerani

sehe manggi geren weceku se deyeme mukdefi tugi talman gese. sergudai fiyanggo geren juse i emgi aisin menggun i gašiha[163] maktame efime bisire namšan emu amba gasha uthai wasime genefi šoforome jafafi den mukdefi gamaha. gūwa juse sabufi gemu golofi sujume boode dosifi han ama de alame ehe oho sergudai ahūn be emu gasha jifi šoforome gamahabi serede ilmun han donjifi ambula fancafi hutu be takūrafi monggoldai nakcu be hūlame gajifi beceme hendume sini gajiha sergudai fiyanggo be emu amba gasha šoforome gamaha. erebe. bi bodoci gemu sini arga be boljoci ojarakū. si minde adarame icihiyambi sehede monggoldai elhei gūnici gūwa waka. nišan saman dere seme uthai hendume ejen ume jili banjire bi gūnici guwa waka weihun gurun de uju tucike. amba gurun de alin algiha nišan saman jifi gamaha dere. bi te uthai amcame genefi tede baime tuwaki. tere saman gūwa de duibuleci ojorakū sefi uthai amcame genehe tereci nišan saman sergudai fiyanggo be bahara jakade ambula urgunjeme gala be jafafi kuteleme amasi marifi fe jugūn be jafame yaburede monggoldai amargici amcame hūlame saman gehe majige aliya. muse giyan be majige gisureki. ekisaka gamara doro bio. mini beye utala hūsun fayame arkan seme gajime baha sergudai fiyanggo be si yargiyan i saman de ertufi bai gamaki sembio aise. meni ilmun han fancafi mimbe wakalahabi. te bi adarame jabumbi. saman gehe elhe i gūnime tuwafi. dade basan geli akū bai gamarangge. elei giyan de acanarakū gese sehede. nišan saman hendume monggoldai si ere gese sain angga baici hono sinde basan majige werimbi. si aika suweni han de ertufi etuhušeme yabuci we sinde gelembio muse emu amba babe acafi. da dube tucibuki sefi ilan dalhan misun. ilan sefere hoošan be buhe

163. S: gacuha

manggi monggoldai geli baime hendume sini bure
basan jaci komso kai jai majige nonggime bureo
sehe manggi nišan saman geli emu ubu nonggime
56 buhe manggi. geli baime hendume ere majige basan be meni han de burede yargiyan i banjinarakū
dade mini weile adarame sume mutembi. bairengge
saman gehe sini gajiha coko indahūn be minde werifi mini weile be sume ilmun han de benefi ini
abalara indahūn akū. dobori hūlara coko akū de
meni han urgunjefi oci emude saman gehe i baita
muyahūn ombi. jaide mini weile be sumbi serede.
nišan saman hendume tere inu juwe ergide tusa
yohi ombi. damu sergudai de jalgan be nonggime
buci ere indahūn coko be gemu werifi genembi sehede monggoldai hendume saman gehe si uttu gisu-
reci sini derebe tuwame orin se jalgan nonggiha.
57 saman hendume oforo niyaki olhoro unde de gamaha
seme tusa akū. tuttu oci gūsin se jalgan nonggire. kemuni gūnin mujilen toktoro undede gamaha seme ai tusa. tuttu oci dehi se jalgan nonggire. kemuni derengge wesihun alire unde de
gamaha seme tusa akū. tuttu oci susai se jalgan
nonggire. kemuni sure mergen ojoro unde gamaha
seme ai tusa. tuttu oci ninju se jalgan nonggire. kemuni niru beri be urebume tacire unde
de gamaha seme tusa akū. tuttu oci nadanju se
jalgan nonggire. kemuni narhūn weile be tacire
unde de gamaha seme ai tusa. tuttu oci jakūnju
se jalgan nonggire. kemuni jalan baita be ulhi-
58 re unde de gamaha seme tusa akū. tuttu oci.
uyunju se jalgan be nonggiha. jai nonggici banjinarakū oho. sergudai ereci amasi ninju aniya
nimeku akū. tanggū aniya targa[164] akū. ura
šurdeme uyun juse ujikini. jalan aššame jakūn
jui sabukini. uju funiyehe sartala[165] angga
weihe sortolo. dara musutele.[166] yasa ilhanara
tala. bethe bekterere teile. umuhu[167] de

164. turga
165. V,S: saratala--terminal converb of *šarambi*.
166. V: musetele--terminal converb of *musembi*.
167. V,S: umuhun

siteme. guweye[168] de hamtame banjikini sehede. nišan saman baniha bume hendume monggoldai nakcu si ere gese gūnin tucime fungneci coko indahūn be gemu buhe. coko be aši seme hūla. indahūn be ceo seme hūla serede monggoldai baniha bume ambula urgunjefi coko indahūn jergi be gaime yaburede gūnime cendeme hūlame tuwaki seme juwe be gemu sindafi. aši aši. ceo ceo seme hūlara jakade coko indahūn gemu amasi marifi aibi seme nišan saman be amcame genehe. monggoldai golofi ergen biakū[169] sujume baihanafi. he fa seme fodome baime saman gehe ainu yobodombi. absi sini coko indahūn be mini hūlara sasa amasi forome genehebi. bairengge ume holtoro ere juwe hacin jaka be gamarakū oci. yargiyan ojorakū. han mimbe wakalahade bi adarame alime mutembi seme dahin dahūn baire de nišan saman injeme hendume heni yobodome fihengge. ereci amasi saikan i eje bi sinde alara. coko be gu gu seme hūla. indahūn be eri eri seme hūla sehe manggi monggoldai hendume gehe heni tani yobodoho. mini beye nei taran tucikebi. sefi saman i alaha gisun songkoi hūlara jakade coko indahūn gemu monggoldai beye be šurdeme uju ucihin[170] lasihime dahalame genehe. tereci nišan saman sergudai gala be jafafi kutuleme jidere be jugūn dalbade ini eigen be ucarafi tuwaci nimenggi mucen be šušu orho i tuwa sindame fuyebumbi. arbun be tuwaci jili banjihabi. sargan be sabure jakade weihe be emgeri katur seme saime seyeme hendume dekdeni[171] nišan si gūwa niyalma be gemu weijubume mutere anggala ajigen ci gaiha haji halhūn eigen mimbe aitubume gamaci eheo bi. cohome ubade nimenggi mucen be fuyebufi simbe aliyambi. si eici aitubure eici aituburakū babe hūdun gisure. yargiyan aituburakū oci simbe unggirakū

59

60

61

168. S: guye

169. = bi akū

170. V,S: uncehen

171. S relates this word to *dekden i gisun* "baseless talk" and *dekdersembi* "to be haughty, to be overweening." Thus, he translates the word as "fickle."

ningge mujanggo.[172] ere mucen uthai sini bakcin oho sehede nišan saman baime hendume

eigen haji.
hailambi šulembi ekšeme donji
hailambi šulembi haha haji
hailambi šulembi hahilame donji
hailambi šulembi nekeliyen šan be
hailambi šulembi neifi donji
62 hailambi šulembi giramin šan be
hailambi šulembi gidafi donjireo
hailambi šulembi sini beye
hailambi šulembi siren sube lakcaha
hailambi šulembi aifini bucefi
hailambi šulembi aikime[173] niyaha
hailambi šulembi giranggi yali
hailambi šulembi gemu hungkenehe[174]
hailambi šulembi absi weijubumbi
hailambi šulembi haji eihen[175]
hailambi šulembi gūsime[176] gūnici
hailambi šulembi dulembume unggireo
hailambi šulembi sini eifu de
hailambi šulembi hoošan jiha be
hailambi šulembi labdu deijire
hailambi šulembi buda sogi be
hailambi šulembi labdu doboro
hailambi šulembi sini eniye
hailambi šulembi eršeme kutulembi
hailambi šulembi erebe gūnici
63 hailambi šulembi ergen be guwebureo
hailambi šulembi sakda eme be
hailambi šulembi šar seme gūnifi
hailambi šulembi hor seme dulembureo
hailambi šulembi

172. S: mujanggao
173. S: akiyame
174. V relates this word to *hungkihe* "to make soft" and S to *honggonoho* "to crumble." V's explanation is more plausible. The basic form is expanded by use of the illative suffix *-ne-*.
175. V,S: eigen
176. V,S: gosime

seme baire de ini eigen weihe be saime seyeme hendume dekdeni baili akū nišan saman sargan si donji mini beye weihun fonde mimbe yadahūn seme yasa gidame fusihūšaha ba umesi labdu kai sini beye mujin i dolo inu getuken i sambi. ere elei gūnin cihai oho dabala sakda eme be sain ehe eršere eršerakū sini gūnin cihai dabala geli yasa de bisireo enenggi. onggolo nergin juwe kimun be emu mudan de sinde karulabuki. eici sini beye nimenggi mucen de dosire eici mini beye 64 simbe aname dosimbure be hahilame toktobu serede saman dere fularafi jili banjime hūlame hendume haji eigen si donji.

denikun denikun si bucerede
denikun denikun aibe werihe
denikun denikun yadara boigon de
denikun denikun sini sakda eniye be
denikun denikun minde werihe
denikun denikun bi kunduleme ujimbi
denikun denikun faššame hiyoošulambi
denikun denikun eihen beye
denikun denikun gūnime tuwa
denikun denikun uthai balingga[177]
denikun denikun niyalma inu kai
denikun denikun mangga mujin be
denikun denikun bi tucibufi
denikun denikun simbe majige
denikun denikun amtalambume tuwaki 65
denikun denikun sini kira[178] mangga be
denikun denikun eberebume tuwaki
denikun denikun umesi bade
denikun denikun unggimbi kai
denikun denikun weceku de baime
denikun denikun bujan be šurdere
denikun denikun amba bulehun[179]
denikun denikun hūdun hahi
denikun denikun mini eihen

177. V,S: bailingga
178. V: giran; S: cira. We have followed the former.
179. V,S: bulehen

denikun denikun šoforome jafafi
denikun denikun fungtu hoton de
denikun denikun maktafi enteheme
denikun denikun tumen jalan de
denikun denikun niyalmai beyede
denikun denikun banjiburakū obuki
denikun denikun

66 ḣūlara de amba bulehun deyeme genefi uthai šoforome jafafi deyeme fungtu hoton de maktaha be saman sabufi den jilgan deyangku be hūlame hendume.

deyangku deyangku eigen akū de
deyangku deyangku encehešeme banjiki
deyangku deyangku haha akū de
deyangku deyangku kangtaršame banjiki
deyangku deyangku eniye hūcihin[180] de
deyangku deyangku efime banjiki
deyangku deyangku se be amcame
deyangku deyangku sebjeleme banjiki
deyangku deyangku juse akū de
deyangku deyangku julesi ome banjiki
deyangku deyangku hala mukūn akū de
deyangku deyangku hajilame banjiki
deyangku deyangku asigan be amcame
deyangku deyangku antahašame banjiki
deyangku deyangku

67 yayame geyeme sergudai fiyanggo i gala be kutuleme edun i adali efime yabume su i adali sujume yabume jihei tuwaci jugūn i dalbade emu taktu be sabubumbi weilehengge umesi horonggo saikan bime. sunja hacin i boconggo tugi borhohobi. nišan saman hanci genefi tuwaci dukai jakade juwe aisin uksin saca etuhe enduri selei maitu jafame ilime tuwakiyahabi. nišan saman hanci genefi baime hendume agusa ere aiba bihe. dolo webi getuken alamburẹo serede tere enduri alame taktu de bisire abdaha sain de arsubure.

180. S: hūncihin

fulhu[181] saide[182] fusubure.[183] omosi mama tehebi. nišan saman baime hendume mini jihe ildun
de mama de hengkileki sembi. yala ombi ojorakū
seme fonjiha de dukai enduri hendume ombi sehede 68
nišan saman ilan sefere hoošan. ilan dalhan
misun baniha bume dosime genehe. jai duka de
isinafi tuwaci inu juwe uksin saca etuhe enduri
tuwakiyahabi. nišan saman dosime generede esukiyeme ilibufi aibi niyalma balai ere duka be
dosimbi hūdun bedere majige notašaci[184] uthai
tantambi serede nišan saman baime amba enduri
ume jili banjire ehe fainggo waka weihun gurun i
nišan saman serengge uthai bi inu jugūn ildun
balingga omosi mama de acafi hengkileki sembi.
juwe enduri hendume tere gese ginggun gūnin oci
dosime genefi hūdun tuci seme alahade nišan saman inu onggolo songkoi baniha basan bufi dosime 69
genehe. ilaci duka de isinafi inu juwe enduri
tuwakiyahabi. inu onggolo songkoi baniha bume
dosifi tuwaci taktu de sunja boco sukdun elde-
šehebi uce šurdeme sukdun jalukabi geli juwe hehe sunja boco ilhangga etuku etufi uce tuwakiyahabi. uju funiyehe be gemu den šošome galade
aisin hiyanglu be jafahabi. emke menggun i fila
jafahabi. emke injeme hendume ere hehe be bi
takara adali si weihun gurun nisihai bira dalin
de tehe nišan saman wako.[185] saman sesulefi[186]
hendume si ainaha niyalma. bi ainame onggoho

181. S: fulehe "root"; V: fulhuren "sprout." Both interpretations are contextually possible. We have followed the former.

182. = sain de

183. V,S: fusebure

184. V suggests that this is to be equated with *aššaci*, conditional of *aššambi* "to move." S believes it may be a distorted and metathesized writing of *ušatambi* "to vex, to plague." Another tenuous possibility is to equate this word with the conditional of *nushūmbi* "to rush (toward), to charge."

185. V,S: wakao

186. S: sesulafi

takarakū serede tere hehe hendume si ainu mimbe takarakūnii.[187] bi cara aniya mama tucire de
70 omosi mama mimbe bulhūn[188] sain seme gajifi beye hanci takūrambi muse emu tokso niyalma adaki boo nari fiyanggo i sargan mimbe gaifi juwe inenggi dorgide mama tucime bucehe kai serede nišan saman teni takafi ambula urgunjeme absi onggohonii[189] seme ucebe neime bufi dosibuha[190] uju· tukiyeme wesihun tuwaci orto[191] i dulimbade emu sakda mama tehebi funiyehe nimanggi gese šeyen dere seme sabumbi yasa kumsuhun.[192] angga amba. dere golmin. sencehe cokcohūn[193] weihe fularafi tuwaci ojorakū juwe dalbade juwan funcere hehesi ilihabi. juse jajihangge.[194] tebeliyehengge. ome tonggo ulmirengge.[195] ajige jui ararengge. ajige jui be iberengge.[196] folho[197] de teburengge tebumbi. meiherehengge. meiherembi. gamarangge
71 gamambi. gemu šolo akū. šun dekdere ergi uce be tucimbi. nišan saman sabufi ferguweme nade niyakūrafi ilan ilan uyun jergi hengkilefi omosi mama fonjime si ai niyalma bihe. bi ainu takarakū. balai ere bade dosinjimbi sehede nišan saman niyakūrafi ulame ajige niyalma jalan gurun i nisihai birai dalin de tehe nišan saman serengge uthai ajige niyalma ere emu mudan hanilame jihe jugūn ildun de enduri mama de hengkileme tuwan-

187. V,S: takarakūni. This is the negative form of the verb *takambi* "to know," plus the interrogative particle *ni*.

188. V: bolgon

189. V,S: onggohoni. Cf. fn. 187.

190. S: dosimbuha

191. S: ordo

192. S: kumcuhun

193. V,S: cokcohon

194. S: jajahangge. From the verb *jajambi* "to carry on the back."

195. V,S: ulamirangge. However, there is no verb *ulamimbi* listed in the lexical sources. The word is likely related to *ulambi* "to hand down."

196. Neither V or S propose an explanation for this word. We have understood it as a verb related to *iberelembi* "to advance."

197. fulhū

jiha sehede omosi mama hendume absi onggoho simbe banjibure de si fuhali generakū ofi bi simbe horšome[198] yekse hetebufi siša huwaitafi yemcen jafabufi samdabume efin i gese banjibuha bihe. sini beye giyan i gebu tucire ton ere bade emu mudan isinjire be mini beye toktobufi sain ehe yabure eiten erun be sabubufi jalan de ulhibukini seme toktobuha jai sirame jici ojorakū dade saman. baksi. aha mafa ilire. wesihun derengge ojoro. ehe facuhūn yabure. bayan yadahūn hūlha holo. hoošan[199] toose[200] giyohoto.[201] arki omire. falin[202] neifi jiha efire. hehesi be duwendere.[203] sain ehe be gemu ubaci toktobume unggimbi ere gemu hesebun kai. sefi fejergi niyalma de alame saman be gamafi erun koro. fafun be majige tuwabu sehede. uthai emu hehe jifi saman be hacihiyame yabu mini emgi majige sargašaki seme saman dahame sasa genefi tuwaci emu bujan arsuhangge saikan bime huweki sunja boco borhoho bi saman fonjime ere ai bujan serede alame suweni jalan gurun de mama fudere de bolgo ginggun akū. morin ihan jeke akū ningge fodoho gargan be bilafi fudehe turgunde arsuhangge sain. juse i mama ilha inu sain. tere bujan arsuhangge luku akū bime eden dadan ohongge suweni weihun gurun mama fuderede fodoho gargan ihan morin jeke ningge be baitalaha turgunde juse ilha ehe bime erun sui hūlambi. ere gemu iletu obume tuwaburengge geli yabume šun dekdere ergide emu

72

73

198. V: hurseme. The word should be equated with *hurceme* "to find fault with." Alternation between the consonants -*s*-, -*š*- and -*c*- is common throughout the text.

199. The only meaning given for this word in the standard dictionaries is "paper." However, such a reading makes little sense here. The word should be understood as a mistake for *huwašan* "Buddhist monk." This type of vowel metathesis occurs in various Sibe words.

200. doose

201. V,S: giohoto

202. wali

203. S: dufedere

amba boo dolo emu amba tohoroko[204] fuheŠerede dorgici eiten ujima. feksire gurgu. deyere gasha. nimaha. umiyaha jergi ergengge feniyen feniyen. feksime. deyeme tucirengge lakcan akū. erebe saman sabufi fonjire jakade alame ere eiten ergengge be banjibure ba inu. geli yabume
74 tuwaci emu amba hutu[205] furdan duka be lakcan akū hutu fainggo yabumbi. dolosi tuwaci fungtu hoton i sahaliyan talman borhohobi. donjici dolo hutu songgoro jilgan ambula bi. geli ehe indahūn i gašan. šurdeme niyalmai yali be indahūn tatarame jembi hūlimbure ebubun boo i dolo koro gosihūn[206] be hūlame songgoro jilgan na durgidumbi.[207] geli genggiyen buleku alin. farhūn buleku hada jergi bade. sain ehe erun be getuken i faksalambi. geli emu yamun be sabumbi. tanggin de emu hafan tefi geren fainggo be beidembi. wargi ashan boode lakiyahangge hūlha tabcin jergi erun niyalma sa be horihabi. dergi hetu boode horihangge ama eme de hiyoošun akū.
75 eihen sargan jurgan akū. urse be selgelehebi.[208] geli tuwaci ama eme be toore tantaha ningge be nimenggi mucen de carume erulembi. šabi sefu be hūlahame[209] toohangge be tura de hūwaitafi gabtame erulembi. sargan eigen be hatarangge be faitarame erulembi. doose hehe de latume yabuhangge ging be natahūraha[210] seme ilan gargan šaka i šakalame erulembi. bele ufan sisābume talahangge be hujureku mose[211] de gidame erulembi

204. V,S: tohorokū

205. S interprets the word as it stands. *Hoton* "city" makes better contextual sense. The word may have been misspelled in anticipation of the term *hutu* "ghost," which appears shortly after this word.

206. V,S: gosihon

207. V,S: durgedumbi

208. S suggests that this is a verb formed from *selhen* "cangue."

209. hūlhame

210. S: nantuhūraha

211. S: this is a shortened form of *moselakū* "millstone." It has been abbreviated under the influence of Chinese *mo-shih* 磨石

habšan be belehe. holbon be efulehe ningge be
sele futa be fulgiyan šerebufi halabume erulembi.
hafan tefi ulintuhe ningge be dehe i yali be deheleme erulembi. juwe eigen gaihangge be faita-
kū faksa hūwalame erulembi. eigen be toohangge
yelenggu[212] be faitame erulembi. uce fangkara
ningge be gala be hadame erulembi. hūlhame gi- 76
gun[213] donjirengge be šan be fade hadame erulembi hūlha holo be yabuhangge selei mukšan i tan-
tame erulembi hehe beye bolhūn akū giyang ula de
ebšehe[214] ningge. ice tofohon inenggi de natu-
hūn[215] be ofoho[216] ningge be duranggi muke be
omibume erulembi. sakdasi sabe hirahangge be
yasa be deheleme erulembi. anggasi. sargan jui
duwendehe ningge be tuwa tura de nikebume halabume erulembi. daifu okto fudasi omibufi buce-
buhe ningge. daifu i hefelii[217] be secime erulembi. hehe eigen baiha hūlhame latume yabuhangge
be suhe ci yali be sacime erulembi. geli tuwaci
emu amba omo de aisin menggun dooha[218] cahabi.
dele yaburengge gemu sain be yabuha hūturingga
urse. tuišun[219] sele ciyoo de yaburengge gemu 77
ehe be yabuha urse be hutu šaka gidai i gidalame
tuhebufi meihe jabjan de šeribumbi. dooha ujande
ehe indahūn alifi niyalmai yali senggi jeme omime kemuni niosihūn[220] serakū[221] sembi. dooha i
dalbade emu pusa enduri de tefi gala de nomun be
jafafi hūlame donjibumbi. tafulara bithei gisun
ehe be yabuci bucehe gurun de erun sui hūlambi.
sain be yabuci erun hūlarakū bime uju jergi niyalma fucihi ejen tembi. jai jergi gung i dolo
banjinambi. ilaci jergi gurun efu taiši hafan

212. S: ilenggu
213. V,S: gisun
214. S: ebišehe
215. S: nantuhūn
216. S: oboho
217. V,S: hefeli
218. V,S: doohan
219. S: teišun
220. miosihūn
221. sarakū--negative of *sambi* "to know."

jergi tembi. duici jergi jiyanggiyūn amban tembi. sunjaci jergi bayan wesihun ombi. ningguci jergi baisin niyalma giyohoto de banjinambi.
78 nadaci jergi eihen lorin morin ihan jergi. banjinambi. jakūci jergi gasha gurgu de banjinambi. uyuci jergi aihama.[222] nimaha ubaliyame banjinambi. juwanci jergi beten. umiyaha yerhu[223] jergi ubaliyame banjinambi. seme den jilgan i hūlame donjibume tafulambi. geren erunbe nišan saman tuwame wajifi amasi taktu de jifi omosi mama de hengkileme acafi. mama alame jalan gurun de isinaha manggi geren urse ulhibume ala sefi. uthai hengkileme fakcafi nišan saman sergudai be kutuleme da jihe jugūn ci jime fulgiyan bira dalin de isinjifi. bira ejin de basan bume yemcen be bira de maktafi saman sergudai be gaime ninggude ilifi doome cargi dalin de isinjifi. geli yabume goidahakū doholo laihi
79 dogūn de isinjifi onggolo yabuha be dahame takara jakade hendume saman isinjiha yargiyan i mangga saman seci ombi. baldu bayan i jui sergudai fiyanggo be bahafi gajihangge ecehen muten ajigen akū ereci ele gebu tucimbi kai sefi weihu de tafa seme hacihiyafi saman sergudai be gaime weihu de tafame tefi doholo laihi hontoho selbi selbime dartai dome dalin de isinjifi weihu ci wasifi basan bume baniha arafi fe jugūn be jafame yabume goidahakū baldu bayan i boode isinjifi. da jari nari fiyanggo uthai orin damgin muke be oforo šurdeme dulaha.[224] dehi hunio muke be dere šurdeme dulafi.[225] hiyan be jafafi
80 baime aitubume gelabure gisun i yayahangge.

ke keku keku ere yamji
keku dengjan la be

222. It is interesting that both V and S fail to transcribe this word. It should be equated with *aihūma* "turtle."

223. V,S: yerhuwe

224. S: doolaha

225. S: doolafi

keku gida nufi[226]
keku ainaha algin
keku weinehe welgin[227]
keku halai hashūri
keku yala yashūri[228]
keku bayari hala
keku abdaha de arsuha
keku fulehe de fusuhe[229]
keku sergudai fiyanggo
keku abalame genefi
keku nimekulefi bucehe
keku erei turgunde
keku ilan saman ilgaci
keku duin saman dekeneci[230]
keku ere fainggo be
keku bucehe gurun
keku ilmun han
keku gamaha sembi
keku erei turgunde
keku nisihai birai
keku dalin de tehe
keku ursu[231] gurun de
keku uju tucike
keku amba gurun de
keku algin tucike
keku ayan hiyan be

226. S suggests that this is the comitative form of *gidambi* "to turn off." The author has incorrectly inserted a space before the comitative suffix *-nu-*.

227. *Weinehe* and *welgin* are fashioned by fusing *we* "who" to *ainaha* "what sort of" and *algin* "fame." An alliterative pair results that is parallel to the previous line.

228. The meaning of *yashūri* and *hashūri* are unknown. They may be special clan terms. Note that these two lines also have internal alliteration and are parallel to one another.

229. V,S: fusehe

230. S relates this to *dengnembi* "to balance, to compete with, to weigh."

231. V,S: urse

keku jafame gaifi
81 keku alin be dabame
keku amcame genefi
keku algin be gaihade
keku jorime tuwaha
keku adališara jakade
keku baime gajifi
keku ineku yamji de
keku farhūn bade
keku fayanggo be fargaha
keku ehe bade
keku ergen be ganaha bihe
keku amasi marime jifi,
keku lelii[232] fodoho
keku da gargan de
keku dalaha daimin
keku adame gargan de
keku alha daimin
keku alin be šurdere
keku aisin inggalii
keku mukden be šurdere
keku menggun inggalii
keku taran tasha
keku oniku lefu
keku jakūn da jabjan
keku uyun da meihe
keku cakūra moo falga
keku jakūn juru manggi
keku mang moo falga
keku juwan juru manggi
keku weijubume jiki
keku aitubume gaiki
keku gele[233] gete
keku

82 sefi nišan saman šurgeme deribufi gaitai ilifi yayame deribuhe yabuha babe gamaha turgun be tucibume yayara gisun.

232. V: leli
233. gela--imperative of *gelambi* "to wake up."

deyangku deyangku geren niyalma jari
donji
deyangku deyangku baldu bayan sini
beye
deyangku deyangku emke emken donji bai
deyangku deyangku sini jui be
deyangku deyangku aisin hiyanglu de
deyangku deyangku tebume gajiha
deyangku deyangku šoforo de šoforome
deyangku deyangku gajime jihe kai
deyangku deyangku boobai oho de
deyangku deyangku hafirame gajiha
deyangku deyangku bucehe beyede
deyangku deyangku weijubuhebi
deyangku deyangku fayangga be oron
beyede
deyangku deyangku singgebume sindahabi
deyangku deyangku omosi mama de baiha
kerani kerani ereci amasi
kerani kerani nimeku yangšan
kerani kerani akū obume
kerani kerani banjikini sehe 83
kerani kerani uyunju se jalgan
kerani kerani ulgun[234] be tolome
kerani kerani uyun juse ujikini
kerani kerani gamaha ilmun han de
kerani kerani coko indahūn be
kerani kerani baili de werihe
kerani kerani basan jergi be
kerani kerani omosi mama de
kerani kerani hengkileme acaha
kerani kerani sini jui de
kerani kerani geli enen baiha
kerani kerani jalan de ulhibure
kerani kerani mama eršere de
kerani kerani ginggun bolgo i
kerani kerani mama ilha sain
kerani kerani damu sain be
kerani kerani ehe be yabuci

234. urgun

kerani kerani eiten erun iletu
kerani kerani gemu getuken sabuha
kerani kerani mini eigen mimbe
kerani kerani aitubu seme
84 kerani kerani baire jakade
kerani kerani mini gisun oci
kerani kerani yali sube niyaha
kerani kerani weijubure de mangga
kerani kerani mini eigen fancafi
kerani kerani nimenggi mucen de
kerani kerani mimbe carume wambi
kerani kerani erei turgunde
kerani kerani mini wecen šoforofi
kerani kerani fungtu hoton de
kerani kerani maktafi enteheme
kerani kerani niyalmai beye banjiburakū
kerani kerani geli geren hutu
deyangku deyangku fainggo se
deyangku deyangku aitubu seme
deyangku deyangku siran i baime
deyangku deyangku jugūn be heturefi
deyangku deyangku bairengge jilaka
deyangku deyangku jaci labdu kai
deyangku deyangku labdu basan werihe
deyangku deyangku geren dekdehe
85 deyangku deyangku teni waliyame jihe
deyangku deyangku

sefi uthai oncohūn[235] fahabuha be da jari geli hiyan ci oforo šurdeme fangsifi[236] teni gelahabi. amala saman beye sergudai fiyanggo oron beyede fainggo be feshure[237] jakade dartai aitufi bekene[238] luduru sere[239] jilgan gisun gisureme

235. S: oncohon

236. S: fangsafi

237. V has *feshelere* "to kick": S, *fushere* "to fan." The latter interpretation, which posits simple vowel metathesis, is more probable.

238. V equates this with *beki* "strong"; S with *bekiken* "rather strong." The word is probably related to this family.

239. V,S: ludur sere

muke emu moro bureo serede. gajifi buhe manggi
omifi hendume emu amba amu amgafi kejine tolgiha
sefi uthai ubaliyame tefi. booi urse urgunjefi.
teni turgun be sergudai de alara jakade teni
bucehe be safi nišan saman gehede hengkileme
banihalara de baldu bayan falanggo dume injefi
inu dorolome hendume yarigiyan i enduri saman.
gehe kesi de mini jui dahūme aituha akū bici
fulehe lakcame bihe seme beye etuku be jafafi 86
saman de etubume cusile gu tetun i hūntaha[240] de
jalu nure tebufi niyakūrafi aliburede. nišan
saman hūntaha be alime gaifi sekiyembume[241] omifi karu doro arame hendume ere inu yuwan wai
hūturi de teni muyahūn icihiyame ohobi. ere
uthai juwe ergide geren sasa gemu hūturi kai.
yuwan wai geli amba bolosu hūntaha de jalu nure
tebufi jari de inu alibume hendume fulu singgi-
yabuha bilga[242] monggo[243] akšabuha nure ci majige gidame omireo serede. nari fiyanggo nure be
alime gaifi omimbime hendume ai joboho babi.
tehe baci aljaha akū de joborakū gese aika jobo- 87
ci saman gehe fulu joboho bucehe gurun de emu
marin yabuha be dahame ambula šadaha dere. saman injeme hendume fiyanggo deo jari si donji
dekdeni yoro gisun de ilan fun saman seci. nadan fun i sain jari akū oci banjinarakū sehebi
kai. geren donjifi gemu ambarame injecehe bi.
amala lo yuwan wai ahalji bahalji juwe aha be
hūlafi alame ihan morin honin ulgiyan jergi adun
data sade gemu ala. adun tome dulin dendefi
belhe saman gehe baili de karulame beneki seme
uthai sarin belhefi ambarame omime sarilara de
gemu ambula soktoho amala deren be bederebufi
sejen morin belhefi. jiha menggun etuku adu
jergi be inu dulin dendeme banjibufi sejen de te- 88
bufi. jari de etuku emu yohi yalure akta emke.

240. V,S: hūntahan

241. V,S: sekiyebume--causative of *sekiyembi* "to filter."

242. S: bilha

243. V,S: monggon

enggemu hadala yongkiyan. menggun juwe tanggū yan banjibufi saman jari sasa jaka suwaliyame boode benebuhe amala nišan saman ambula bayan oho nari fiyanggo i emgi haji baita be inu nakafi beyebe toktobume tob tondo obufi banjimbi demun i dufen[244] baita de lasha obuhabi. saman geren erun hacin be sabufi teni mujin nitarahabi. emu fi de julergi miosihūn ehe jergi be toncihiyame[245] arahabi. deranggi[246] muke singifi[247] genggiyen bolgo oho muke gese. ere babe bithe donjire agutasa gehetese kimcici ombi kai. nišan saman i emge[248] amala toksoi urse leole-
89 cerengge ere mudan saman hanilame genehe bade ini eigen be sabufi inbe[249] aitubu seme baiha. aika mimbe aituburakū oci nimenggi mucen de ini sargan be carume wambi sehede nišan saman ini weceku de ertufi. eigen be šoforofi fungtu hoton de maktaha sembi. ere jergi gisun be amala saman i emge donjifi jili banjifi urun be hūlafi da turgun be fonjihade urun i gisun ini beye mimbe aitubu sembi. mini gisun yali niyaha sube lakcaha aituburede mangga sehede. uthai urun be nimenggi mucen de carume wambi serede mini weceku šoforofi fungtu hoton de maktahangge yargiyan sehede emge hendume tuttu oci si eigen be dahūme waha kai. si olime jailaci ai ojorakū. absi gūnin mangga sefi. gemun hecen de
90 genefi ioi ši hafan de habšafi. yamun ci nišan saman be selgiyeme gajifi dahin jabun gaici ini emge alibume habšaha bithe ci encu akū ofi.

244. V,S: dufe

245. S suggests a relationship to *tongkimbi* "to outline." According to such an interpretation, the velar has palatalized under the influence of the high front vowel *-i-*, and the verb has been expanded by reference to the common alternation of *-i-* and *-hiya-* (cf. *tacimbi* and *tacihiyambi*).

246. V: duranggi

247. V,S: singgefi

248. V,S: emhe

249. V,S: imbe--object form of third person pronoun.

jabun be bukdarun weilefi da turgun be tucibume ejen de wesimbuhede hese ambula jili banjifi. beidere jurgan de afabufi ini weile de tehere-bume kooli songkoi icihiya sehe. jurgan ci we-simbuhe gisun buhime uladuha[250] baita de nišan saman gidahakū be tuwaci inu emu hehei i dolo baturu seci ombi. emgeri jabun alime gaiha be dahame ergen toodabuci inu ombi. sehede tai-tsung hūwangdi hese wasimbume uthai ini eigen i songkoi ceni gašan de bisire hocin[251] dolo saman yekse siša yemcen agūra be suwaliyama emu pijan de tebufi sele futa ci akdulame hūwaitafi hocin de makta mini hese akū oci ume tucibure seme wasimbuha de ioi ši hafan songkoi icihiyame gamahabi. ere amala lo yuwan wai jui sergudai fiyanggo inu ini ama i yabuha be alhūdame yada-hūn be wehiyeme akū de aisilame sain yabufi juse omosi jalan jalan wesihun hafan jiha menggun ambula bayan wenjeshūn[252] ohobi. ere uthai sain da deribun bithe ofi geren de ulhibuhe. udu tuttu bicibe amba doro de dosirakū miosihūn ta-cihiyan baita. amala urse alhūdaci ojorakū. eteme targaki mentuhun mini majige amba muru nišan saman bithe be tuwahangge. jaci aniya gi-yalabufi goidaha de yargiyan i gemu onggohobi. eden dadun[253] ba umesi labdu. sara babe gūnime fisembume arahangge yargiyan yokta[254] gese aika gūwa baci yongkiyan sain ningge bahaci ere bit-hede jukime araci inu ombi. erei jalin oros gurun wargi[255] amba tacikū i manju bithe tacibure

91

92

250. V,S: ulanduha
251. V,S: hūcin
252. S: wenjehun
253. eden dadan
254. yokto
255. The author was actually an instructor at the Russian Oriental Institute in Vladivostok, which was not in the "West," as the use of *wargi* would indicate. However, in the Sibe dialect the words for "East" and "West" are just the opposite from those in standard written Manchu [Yamamoto 1969:129]. The author may have been confused by the Sibe forms or some other Manchu dialect that had this feature.

sefu dekdengge i baime alarangge gerbincyrgufu
ge looye i baci sibkime tuwafi eden ekiyehun ba
bici wesihun galai fi jafafi nonggime fisembureo
erei jalin donjibume arahabi.

Bibliography

Aberle, David F. 1952. "'Arctic Hysteria' and Latah in Mongolia." *Transactions of the New York Academy of Science*, Series 2. 14, no. 7: 291-97.

Artscanada. 1973/1974. *Stones, Bones, and Skin: Ritual and Shamanic Art*.

Bogoraz, Vladimir [Waldemar Bogoras]. 1910. "K psikhologii shamanstva u narodov severo-vostochnoi Azii." *Etnograficheskoe obsor-eniye* 94-95: 1-36.

Boon, James. 1973. *From Symbolism to Structural-ism: Lévi-Strauss in a Literary Tradition*. New York: Harper & Row.

Chin Shu 晉書 [Records of the Chin dynasty]. 1969. *Erh-shih-wu shih* 二十五史 [The twenty-five dynastic histories]. Tai-pei: K'ai-ming Bookstore.

Ch'ing-wen tsung-hui 清文總彙 [Manchu-Chinese dictionary]. 1897.

Diószegi, Vilmos. 1960. "Schmanlieder der Mandschu." *Acta Orientalia* 11: 84-104.

Eliade, Mircea. 1961. *Images and Symbols*. Translated by Philip Mairet. New York: Sheed & Ward.

———. 1964. *Shamanism: Archaic Techniques of Ecstasy*. Translated by Willard R. Trask. Princeton: Princeton University Press.

Findeisen, Hans. 1957. *Schamentum: Dargestellt am Beispiel Bessenheits-priester nordeurasiatischer Völker*. Stuttgart: W. Kohlhammer Verlag.

Foucault, Michel. 1973. *The Order of Things* (A translation of *Les Mots et les choses*). New York: Vintage Books.

Foulks, Edward F. 1972. *The Arctic Hysterias*. Washington, D.C.: American Anthropological Association.

Fuchs, Walter. 1943. "Der Jesuiten-Atlas der Kanghsi-Zeit." *Monumenta Serica*, vol. 4. Peking: Fu-jen Universität.

Geertz, Clifford. 1971. "Religion as a Cultural System." In *Anthropological Approaches to the Study of Religion*. Edited by Michael Banton. A.S.A. Monographs 3: 1-46.

Grunwedel, Albert. 1970. *Mythologie des Buddhismus*. 1900. Osnabrück: Otto Zeller Verlag.

Haenisch, Erich. 1961. *Mandschu Grammatik*. Leipzig: VEB Verlag Enzyklopädie.

Han i araha nonggime toktobuha manju gisun i buleku bithe [Manchu dictionary compiled by imperial decree]. 1708.

de Harlez, Charles. 1887. *La religion nationale des Tartares orientaux: Mandchous et Mongols, comparée à la religion des anciens Chinois, d'après les texts indigènes, avec le rituel tartare de l'empereur K'ien-Long traduit pour la première fois*. Louvain.

Harner, Michael J. 1973. *Hallucinogens and Shamanism*. London: Oxford University Press.

Hauer, Erich. 1952. *Handwörterbuch der Mandschusprache*. 3 vols. Wiesbaden: Otto Harrassowitz.

Hoffmann, Helmut. 1967. *Symbolik der Tibetischer Religionen und des Schamanismus*. Stuttgart: Anton Hiersemann.

Hsin-hua tsu-tien 新華字典 [New Chinese dictionary]. 1958. Hong Kong: Hsin Min-chu Press.

Hultkranz Åke. 1970. "Book reviews: 'Anthropological Approaches to Religion.'" *History of Religions* 9: 337-52.

Jenson, Adolf E. 1963. *Myth and Cult among Primitive Peoples*. 1951. Translated by Marianna Tax Choldin and Wolfgang Weissleder. Chicago: University of Chicago Press.

Krotkov, N.N. n.d. "Kratkie zametki o sovremennom sostoienii shamanstva u sibo, zhivushchikh v Iliiskoi oblasti i Tarbagatae." *Zapiski vostochnogo otdela russkogo arkheologicheskogo obshchestva* 21: 117-36.

Langlès, Louis. 1804. *Rituel des Tatars-Mantchoux, rédigé par l'ordre de l'empereur Kien Long, et précedé d'un discours préliminaire composé par ce souverain; avec les dessins des principaux ustensiles et instrumens du culte chamanique*. Paris.

Lattimore, Owen. 1967. *Inner Asian Frontiers of China*. Boston: Beacon Press.

Laufer, Berthold. 1917. "Origin of the Word Shaman." *American Anthropologist* 19: 361-71.

Lévi-Strauss, Claude. 1960. "La Structure et la

forme." *Cahiers de l'Institut de science économique appliquée* 9, série M, no. 7: 3-36. Paris: ISEA.

———. 1966. *The Savage Mind.* 1962. Chicago: University of Chicago Press.

———. 1967. *Structural Anthropology.* 1958. Translated by Claire Jacobson and Brooke Grundfest Schoepf. New York: Anchor Books.

———. 1967a. "The Effectiveness of Symbols." 1949. In *Structural Anthropology.*

———. 1967b. "The Sorcerer and His Magic." 1949. In *Structural Anthropology.*

———. 1968. "The Story of Asdiwal." *The Structural Study of Myth and Totemism.* 1958. Edited by Edmund Leach. A.S.A. Monographs 5: 1-47.

———. 1969a. *The Elementary Structures of Kinship.* 1949. Translated by James Harle Bell, John Richard von Sturmer and Rodney Needham. Boston: Beacon Press.

Lommel, Andreas. 1967. *Shamanism: The Beginnings of Art.* 1965. Translated by Michael Bullock. New York: McGraw-Hill Book Co.

Lowie, Robert. 1937. *The History of Ethnographic Theory.* New York: Holt, Rinehart & Winston.

Michael, Franz. 1942. *The Origin of Manchu Rule in China.* Baltimore: Johns Hopkins Press.

Mironov, N. D. and S. M. Shirokogoroff. 1923. "Sramana-Shaman: Etymology of the Word 'shaman.'" *Journal of the Royal Asiatic Society* (Shanghai) 54: 105-30.

Morohashi, Tetsuji 諸橋轍次. 1955-1960. *Dai kanwa jiten* 大漢和辭典 [The great Chinese-Japanese dictionary]. Tokyo.

Narr, Karl J. 1959. "Bärenzeremoniell und

Schamanismus in der Ältern Steinzeit Europas." *Saeculum* 10: 233-72.

Norman, Jerry. 1967. *A Manchu-English Dictionary*. Taipei.

———. 1974. "A Sketch of Sibe Morphology." *Central Asiatic Journal* 18: 159-74.

Peeters, Hermes. 1940. *Manjurische Grammatik. Monumenta Serica*, vol. 5. Peking.

Popov, A. A. 1932. *Materialy dlya bibliografii russkoi literatury po izucheniyu shamanstva severno-aziatskikh narodov*. Leningrad: Academia nauk.

Rank, Gustav. 1962. "Shamanism as a Research Subject." In *Studies in Shamanism*. Edited by Carl-Martin Edsman. Stockholm: Almqvist and Wiksell.

Reischauer, Edwin O., and Fairbank, John K. 1960. *East Asia: The Great Tradition*. Boston: Houghton Mifflin.

Rossi, Ino. 1974. "Structuralism as Scientific Method." In *The Unconscious in Culture*. Edited by Ino Rossi. New York: E. P. Dutton & Co.

Rudnev, Andrei. 1912. "Novyia dannyia po Zhivoi mandzhurskoi rechi i shamanstvu." *Otdel'nyi ottisk iz zapisok vostochnago otdeleniia imperatorskago russkago arkehelogicheskago obshchestva* 21: 1-36.

Schmidt, Wilhelm. 1955. *Der Ursprung der Gottesidee*, vol. 12. Münster: Aschendorffsche Verlagsbuchhandlung.

Schröder, Dominik. 1955. "Zur Struktur des Schamanismus." *Anthropus* 50: 849-81.

Sebag, Lucien. 1965. "Le chamanisme ayoréo."

L'Homme 5: 5-32; 92-122.

Seong Baeg-in. 1974. *Nišan Samani Bithe: a Tale of the Manchu Nišan Shaman*. Seoul: Myong-ji University Press.

Shirokogoroff, Sergei M. 1924. *Social Organization of the Manchus*. Shanghai: Royal Asiatic Society, North China Branch. Extra vol. 3.

———. 1929. *Social Organization of the Northern Tungus*. Shanghai: Commercial Press.

———. 1935. *Psychomental Complex of the Tungus*. London: Kegan Paul, Trench, Trübner & Co.

Shweder, Richard A. 1972. "Aspects of Cognition in Zinacanteco Shamans: Experimental Results." In *Reader in Comparative Religion: An Anthropological Approach*. Edited by William A. Lessa and Evon Z. Vogt. New York: Harper & Row.

Silverman, Julian. 1967. "Shamans and Acute Schizophrenia." *American Anthropologist* 69: 21-31.

Tamura, Jitsuzo, Imanishi Shunju, and Sato Hsiashi. 1966. *Wu-t'i ch'ing-wen chien* 五體清文鑑 [Dictionary of the five official Ch'ing languages]. Kyoto: Institute for Inland Asian Studies.

Van der Leeuw, Gerhard. 1963. *Religion in Essence and Manifestation: A Study in Phenomenology*. Translated by J. E. Turner. 1933. New York: Harper & Row.

Volkova, Maria Petrovna. 1961. *Nishan' Samani Bitkhe*. Moscow: Akademia nauk SSSR, Institut narodov Azii.

Wasson, R. Gordon. 1968. *Soma, Divine Mushroom of Immortality*. Ethno-Mycological Studies, no. 1. New York: Harcourt Brace Jovanovich.

Yamamato, Kengo. 1969. *A Classified Dictionary of Spoken Manchu*. Tokyo: Institute for the Study of Languages and Cultures of Asia and Africa.

Zakharov, Ivan. 1875. *Polnyi Man'chzhrusko-Russkii Slovar* [Complete Manchu-Russian dictionary]. St. Petersburg.

Zelenin, Dimitri. 1936. *Kul't ongonov v Sibiri: perezhitki totemisma v ideologii sibirskikh narodov* [The cult of the 'ongens' in Siberia: survivals of totemism in the ideology of the Siberian people]. Trudy instituta antropologii arkheologii i etnografii, vol. 14. Moscow/Leningrad: Izdatel'stvo akademii nauk SSSR.

Index